Tapestry of Hope

Holocaust Writing for Young People

COMPILED BY

LILLIAN BORAKS-NEMETZ & IRENE N. WATTS

60604

Tundra Books

Published in Canada by Tundra Books,
481 University Avenue, Toronto, Ontario M5G 2E9

Published in the United States by Tundra Books of Northern New York,
P.O. Box 1030, Plattsburgh, New York 12901

Library of Congress Control Number: 2002114710

National Library of Canada Cataloguing in Publication

Tapestry of hope : Holocaust writing for young people /
compiled by Lillian Boraks-Nemetz and Irene N. Watts.

ISBN 0-88776-638-2

1. Holocaust, Jewish (1939-1945) – Literary collections.
I. Boraks-Nemetz, Lillian, 1933- II. Watts, Irene N., 1931-

D804.3.T36 2002   C810.8'0358   C2002-905315-3

We acknowledge the financial support of the Government of Canada
through the Book Publishing Industry Development Program (BPIDP)
and that of the Government of Ontario through the Ontario Media
Development Corporation's Ontario Book Initiative. We further
acknowledge the support of the Canada Council for the Arts and the
Ontario Arts Council for our publishing program.

Design: Terri Nimmo

Printed and bound in Canada

1 2 3 4 5 6   08 07 06 05 04 03

For Jennifer, Alex, and Willy
LBN

For Adam, Matthew, and Jean-Michel
INW

ACKNOWLEDGMENTS

The editors thank the Vancouver Holocaust Child Survivor Group of B.C. and acknowledge the ongoing creative educational programming of Roberta Kremer and Frieda Miller. We also thank the Holocaust Education Centre for its inspirational exhibit "We Were Children Then," curated by Viviane Gosselin. Special thanks to Angela Rebeiro, Publisher, Playwrights Canada Press.

CONTENTS

INTRODUCTION

by Kathy Lowinger

If the Holocaust were about evil alone, it would be best to shut its memory away, and never breathe its name. But if the Holocaust is about immeasurable suffering, it is also about courage. If it is about despair, it is also about hope. If it is about needless death, it is also about precious life.

Among the things I treasure the most are two tiny cracked photos. One is of a curly-haired boy, about four years old, clutching a truck as he squints into the sun. The other is of a boy hardly more than a baby. He is perched, laughing, on the running board of a car. They are my brothers, Robert and Paul. They died five years before I was born, and all that remains of them are the photos, their names inscribed in one of Auschwitz's carefully kept ledgers, and a memory that is older than I am. Now that everyone in my parents' generation is dead, I am probably the only person alive who remembers that once there were two little boys who loved trucks and cars, and were dressed up to have their pictures taken on a sunny summer day long ago. They trod so lightly and vanished in smoke.

Because I am the keeper of those brief lives, I understand the feeling of urgency in each contribution to *Tapestry of Hope*. There are so many lives to set down before time sweeps them out of reach, so many acts of courage and faith to share before they are forgotten. Through their stories, poems, and personal accounts, the contributors to *Tapestry of Hope* record the darkest of times, not to dismay us but to show us that nothing can extinguish the spark that gives dignity to life.

I have always been inspired by the great Hungarian freedom fighter and poet, Hannah Szenes. She was tortured and executed by the Hungarian police in November 1944, when she was only twenty-three years old. Hannah Szenes wrote many poems including "Blessed is the Match." In it she calls upon us all to be like a simple match: even as we are consumed, we can defeat the darkness with our light.

Each of the writers you will meet in *Tapestry of Hope* knows about darkness. Each of the stories they share has to do with the darkness, it is true, but also with what counts: lighting the matches of hope that chase the night away.

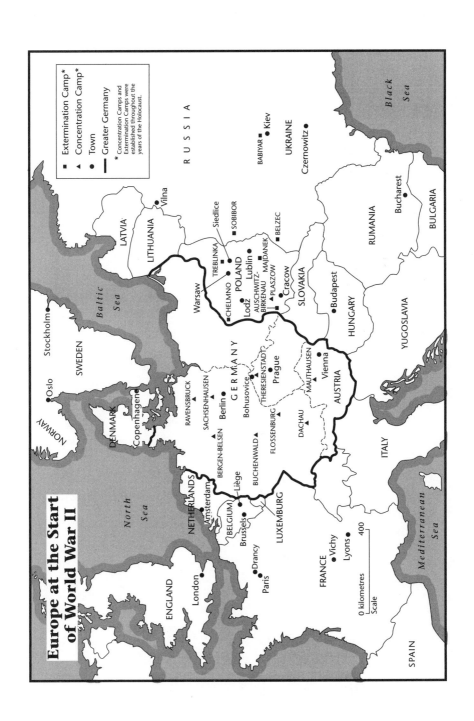

Europe at the Start of World War II

Legend:
- ■ Extermination Camp*
- ▲ Concentration Camp*
- ● Town
- — Greater Germany
- * Concentration Camps and Extermination Camps were established throughout the years of the Holocaust.

Seas and bodies of water: Black Sea, Baltic Sea, North Sea, Mediterranean Sea

Countries: RUSSIA, LATVIA, LITHUANIA, UKRAINE, RUMANIA, BULGARIA, POLAND, SLOVAKIA, HUNGARY, YUGOSLAVIA, GERMANY, AUSTRIA, ITALY, SWEDEN, NORWAY, DENMARK, NETHERLANDS, BELGIUM, LUXEMBURG, FRANCE, ENGLAND, SPAIN

Towns and camps: Vilna, Siedlce, SOBIBOR, TREBLINKA, BELZEC, Warsaw, CHELMNO, Lodz, Lublin, MAJDANEK, PLASZOW, Cracow, AUSCHWITZ-BIRKENAU, Budapest, Bucharest, BABIYAR, Kiev, Czernowitz, Stockholm, Oslo, Copenhagen, RAVENSBRUCK, SACHSENHAUSEN, Berlin, Bohusovice, THERESIENSTADT, Prague, MAUTHAUSEN, Vienna, BERGEN-BELSEN, BUCHENWALD, FLOSSENBURG, DACHAU, Liège, Amsterdam, Brussels, Drancy, Paris, London, Vichy, Lyons

Scale: 0 kilometres — 400

CHILD SURVIVORS
From *Ghost Children*

by Lillian Boraks-Nemetz
For the Child Survivors of the Holocaust

I drift among you
my brothers and sisters
a shadow of myself
a wisp of memory
recycling fragments
of an anguished past

in this room
we recall as in a seance
our former selves
denied a childhood

your voices
come out of the cellars
and the attics of time
and frozen nightmares
murmurings that stir
even these foreign walls
with sounds of guns
and death rattling
in the camps
and ghettoes
that God forgot
and in His forgetfulness
left us with a ghostly memory

Child Survivors

you my sister
recall your shame
at having stolen bread
when your body ached with hunger
and you my sister
with helpless anger
watched a sibling die

and you my brother
lived in hiding
without your parents
while you my brother
died in Auschwitz

no childhood for us then
no schools no gardens
with a dog and cat
no neat kitchens
with mothers baking cakes

only time's catacombs
where we play hide and seek
sustain our memories

Tapestry of Hope

I

Hiding

SURVIVOR STATEMENT

LOUISE STEIN SORENSEN

I was born in Holland in 1929, and lived there with my parents and older sister. I will never forget the panic and the ominous radio announcements that day in May 1940, when German planes flew over our home in Naarden, near Amsterdam. Two years later we were forced into the ghetto. By January 1943 we were separated and hidden by the Dutch underground. For the first six months I was moved around to seven different hiding places. From the late summer of that year until the Canadians liberated us on April 17, 1945, I was hiding in the tiny attic room of a farmworker's house near Apeldoorn, never going outside or seeing other people for almost two years. There were no books or even writing materials available. Eventually my parents joined me there. The first Allied soldier I saw was an Aboriginal Canadian.

TELL NO ONE WHO YOU ARE:

The hidden childhood
of Régine Miller

by Walter Buchignani

Jewish life is full of peril in Nazi-occupied Belgium. The SS arrest Régine's mother and brother. The ten-year-old girl poses as a Gentile child and is forced to change identity constantly. The threat of betrayal is always near. Régine's dearest wish is that someone from her family will survive the war.

Chapter Twenty-one

The tall, narrow house stood on a quiet, tree-lined street that, like Boitsfort, seemed worlds away from the clutter and noise of Brussels. Régine's room was on the upper floor and again it had a view of neighboring homes. But now she shared the room with the two other girls Nicole had told her about.

Nicole had predicted that they could all be friends, and Régine hoped so, too. She looked forward to having other girls to talk to. But as soon as she walked into the room, she had the feeling that Nicole was wrong. The beds of the two girls had been placed side by side at one end of the room while her own bed stood alone at the other end. It did not seem friendly at all. That night as she lay in her new bed, Régine heard the two girls whispering in the dark. They did not want to include her in their conversation.

The next day the girls went out on an errand.

"You're too young to come with us," the first girl said to Régine.

"And you have chores to do," said the second. The girls giggled and walked out the door.

Régine was left behind to make the beds.

In the days that followed, Régine found herself being treated like a servant. She had to change sheets, dust furniture, and scrub floors. By the end of the first week, her hands and knees were covered with calluses.

The hardest room to clean was where Monsieur and Madame Bernard worked. The room was at the back of the house and had two tall chairs and two sinks with mirrors above them. There was also a big hair dryer where women customers sat, reading magazines.

The floor was always covered with hair. No sooner had Régine swept it than she had to start all over again. Customers came and went all day. Régine was expected to stay out of sight when clients were in the house. But as soon as they left, tracking hair all the way to the front door, she was called in to sweep up.

As she swept and scrubbed, Régine felt the eyes of her father watching her. She doubted that he would approve of the work she was expected to do. But then again, she thought if he were here he would probably say it was necessary for the sake of Nicole, who was doing her best to hide Régine from the Germans. She decided not to mention anything when Nicole visited after the first week.

"Are you happy?" Nicole asked, after handing over the pay envelope.

Régine lowered her eyes and uttered a weak "yes."

"Are you sure?"

"Yes," Régine repeated, hiding her despair.

"Good. I'll be back in a few weeks," Nicole told her.

Régine would have liked to rush after her, but instead she stood and watched. She wished that she was still in Boitsfort. Madame André had not been friendly, but she was better than the Bernards. The two girls made Régine feel more lonely than when she had stayed with the solitary old woman.

She was particularly upset because of the Jewish girl. She had hoped to be her friend and wanted to ask her questions. Where was she from? Where were her parents? Why was she staying here? Was she hiding from the Germans, too? But the girl paid no attention to her.

One day, Madame Bernard announced a surprise.

"We're not expecting any customers today," she told Régine. "Why don't we do your hair? Would you like that?"

Régine nodded enthusiastically. She had often wished to change the style of her hair, which was straight and plain. Its auburn color was more red than brown. Adults had always admired the color, but the kids at school used to make fun of her and called her "*roussette*," or redhead.

Her hair had been kept short by her mother so it would be clean and shiny, but it had grown long during the year she had stayed with Madame André.

"How about a permanent?"

A permanent! It was exactly what she had always wished for. Curls!

Régine settled into one of the tall chairs, and Madame Bernard went to work. She tied a large bib around Régine's neck and washed her hair in the sink. Without cutting her hair, she began applying the permanent lotion and putting on the curlers. Then Régine was put under the big dryer.

It took an awfully long time for her hair to dry, or so it seemed to Régine, who was eager to see herself with curls. The dryer was turned off and Régine sat in the tall chair so the curlers could be removed. It seemed to take forever. Was something wrong?

"Almost finished," said Madame Bernard.

"How does it look?" Régine asked. She could not see because the mirror hung on the wall behind her.

"You have to give it some time. That's the way it is with a permanent. After a few days it will look nice."

When the last curler was removed, Régine was handed a small mirror. She brought it up slowly and looked at her reflection. What she saw was worse than she could have imagined. She held the mirror at arm's length for a wider view, but the sight did not improve. She brought her free hand up to her head and grabbed at her hair. The curls were so tight she could not run her hand through it.

"Don't worry," Madame Bernard said. "It'll get better." She looked pleased with herself.

But her hair did not get better. She still could not put a comb through it by the end of her first month when Nicole arrived. She reacted with shock when she saw Régine. She handed over a pay envelope and took Régine aside.

"What did they do to your hair?"

Régine lowered her eyes. She did not want to cause trouble for Nicole. Monsieur and Madame Bernard were standing right behind her.

"It's nothing," she began to say, but her voice cracked.

Nicole bent down and looked into her face. "What's wrong? Tell me."

"It's nothing."

"Is it your hair?" Nicole asked. "Don't worry. It's not that bad. It'll get better."

"It's not that," Régine said, and held out her hands.

Nicole took hold of Régine's hands and her eyes widened. Calluses covered her knuckles completely. The tips of her fingers were cracked and showed traces of dried blood. Her fingernails were broken. Nicole rose and stared at the Bernards. Régine had never seen her so angry.

"Go up to your room," Nicole told Régine. "I have some things to discuss here."

Régine climbed the stairs, wondering if she had done the right thing. Would her father have approved? She sat on the edge of her bed and remembered what he had told her as he sat at his worktable and cut a square of red material into the shape of a star to glue on the back of the yellow Star of David the Germans were forcing them to wear.

"If you are forced to do something you think is wrong," her father had said, "then you must protest." Régine decided she had done the right thing by showing Nicole her hands.

A few days later, Nicole returned. She took Régine aside and told her she had made arrangements for her to stay with another family. That was not all. Nicole said she had something to tell her. She could not explain to her right away, although it was very important.

"Go pack your bag," Nicole told her. "We don't have much time."

What important news did Nicole have for her? Was it about her father? Régine hurried up the stairs. She was relieved to be leaving this household after only one month. She returned downstairs and said a curt good-bye to Monsieur and Madame Bernard. They looked embarrassed.

Nicole was waiting outside. Régine went to join her, passing the two girls who stood watching. She heard them giggle just before the door slammed behind her.

Chapter Twenty-two

Régine boarded the tram and took a seat by the window, with her duffel bag in her lap. She scratched her messy head and waited nervously for Nicole to tell her the important news.

Nicole held her briefcase tightly as she spoke. She had to talk fast, she said, because there was very little time. They were going to the bus station in Brussels. Régine would take a bus that would bring her to a new hiding place in the countryside.

"You understand? It won't be like before," she told Régine. "I won't be able to visit you. It will be too far."

Régine could not hide her disappointment. "You mean, I won't see you?"

"It is only for three months," Nicole said, "and I'll write."

"Where will I be living?"

"In Andoumont," Nicole said. She put her briefcase flat on her lap. "It's a small village in Liège."

Régine had never been to Liège but knew that it was south of Brussels, not far from the Ardennes mountains and the German border. She had learned by heart at the *école primaire* all the nine provinces of Belgium and their capital cities. The capital of the province of Liège was easy to remember because it was also called Liège.

Nicole rummaged inside her briefcase. "It's smaller than Boitsfort. And the people you'll be with live on a farm."

Many children from Brussels had been sent to live in the countryside since the German Occupation began more than three years before. The countryside was safer than the city in the case of bombings and food was more plentiful.

"These people have two children," Nicole said, still rummaging. "So you won't be alone. And you'll be going to school."

"To school?" Régine's eyes lit up at the prospect. "Really?"

"Yes," Nicole said, pulling out an envelope. She looked through the window and frowned. "We're almost there. We're very short of time, so you'll have to listen carefully."

She opened the envelope and pulled out a booklet of ration cards. This certainly could not be the important news. Régine had known about ration cards ever since the beginning of the war. The stamps inside were used for buying vegetables, eggs and milk, and other foods that were rationed and hard to get. The booklet also served as identification. It showed the name, age, and residence of the carrier. Nicole handed the booklet to Régine.

"This is yours," Nicole said.

Régine read the name printed on the booklet. It said Augusta Dubois.

"Who's that?" she asked.

"You," Nicole said.

"Me?"

"This is what I had to tell you," Nicole said. "From now on, you are Augusta Dubois."

"But I'm Régine Miller."

"I know that," said Nicole. "But from now on, no one else must know your real name. What I'm saying is: *Tell no one who you are*. Do you understand? This is very, very important."

Régine nodded, sensing the urgency in Nicole's voice again. "I understand."

"Good. You won't forget? You are Augusta Dubois, not Régine Miller."

"I won't forget. I'm Augusta Dubois."

"And you come from Marche, not Brussels."

"From Marche?" Régine knew that Marche was even farther south than Liège.

"Yes," Nicole said. "Your name is Augusta Dubois and you come from Marche. That's all you have to remember, but it's very important." She paused. "City children are being sent to live on farms. It's part of program called *l'Aide paysanne aux enfants des villes*. Farm families care for children from the city for three months. Understand?"

Régine nodded. She understood very well. It was dangerous to be Jewish under the German Occupation, and the name Augusta Dubois did not sound at all Jewish. Dubois was a safer name than Miller, just like Nicole was a safer name than Fela and blond hair was safer than dark.

"Is that why I can go to school?" Régine tried to look forward to the change.

"Yes. You will attend the same school as Marie, the daughter. They will make all the arrangements," Nicole said.

"How old is Marie?" asked Régine.

"She's nine, two years younger than you. She has an older brother, Jean, who is nineteen."

Nicole looked out the window. "There's the station," she said. "We're here."

Régine saw rows of buses, surrounded by a crowd of children and grown-ups. She slipped the ration book into her duffel bag and felt confused. How would she handle her new, secret identity? What awaited her in Andoumont? She stood up slowly and followed Nicole to the front of the tram.

"Hello," she said to herself, too softly for anyone else to hear. "I'm Augusta Dubois, and," she hesitated for a moment, "and – I come from Marche."

Nicole held Régine's hand and guided her through the crowd. The children were noisy and excited as they hugged their parents. They seemed to be happy to be going to the country, as if it were an adventure. Régine wished she felt the same.

At the end of a long row of buses, Régine and Nicole reached one marked "Liège." The bus was almost full. At the door was a man wearing a ribbon marked *Aide paysanne* and Nicole introduced Augusta Dubois. The man looked at the sheet of paper and nodded: "You are going to Andoumont. Go ahead and get on. I will call your name when we get to your stop."

Nicole bent down and gave her a hug and kiss on the cheek. "Everything will be all right," she said. "Just don't forget what I've told you."

Régine dropped her duffel bag and hugged Nicole with all her might. The she bent down and rummaged through her bag. She pulled out the jar of gooseberry jam that Madame Charles had give her a month before and presented it to Nicole just as the man called out: "Let's go!"

She picked up her duffel bag, gave Nicole a weak smile, and climbed onto the bus.

"Don't forget!" called Nicole.

Régine moved down the bus until she found an empty seat by the window. She sat down with the duffel bag in her lap and looked around. She had not seen so many children in one place since she was forced to leave the *école primaire* more than a year before. The children pressed their faces against the windows and waved to their parents. Régine looked out to Nicole, but did not dare to wave.

The bus began to move. Régine craned her neck and watched Nicole standing on the sidewalk, with her briefcase in one hand and the jar of gooseberry jam in the other. She did not move, even after most of the other grown-ups had begun to walk away. She stood there for as long as Régine could see her.

During the long ride to the countryside, Régine studied the other children on the bus. If they were as afraid as she was, they did not show it. Or were they noisy to mask their fear? Every few miles the bus came to a stop and the man from *Aide paysanne* called out the name of the village and of the children who were to get off.

She now saw a boy sitting across the aisle farther toward the back. She had not noticed him before in the midst of all the noise. He was as quiet as she was. He had red, curly hair and she wished that her permanent had turned into nice curls like his instead of leaving her hair full of knots, which she always felt like scratching.

The boy seemed shy. Every time he caught her looking at him, he turned away. He reminded her of the boy in the window when she was living with Madame André. That boy had been shy, too. He never spoke or waved during their secret through-the-window meetings. Even his smiles were guarded, as if they hid an important truth.

The more she peered at him, the more she felt there was something that set him apart from the children around him. It was the look in his eyes. It showed fear, confusion, anger, and apprehension – the same emotions she was feeling. Yes, Régine thought, the boy must be Jewish.

"Andoumont!" the *Aide paysanne* man called out from the front of the bus, then added a list of names.

Régine placed the duffel bag in the empty seat beside her and stood up. She straightened her coat, picked up her bag, and walked past the boy with the curly, red hair. She caught him looking at her and wondered whether he had guessed her secret, too. Was it so evident? Would others be able to see through her?

She stepped off the bus as Nicole's strange words echoed again in her head: "*Tell no one who you are.*"

HIDDEN CHILDREN:

The Forgotten Survivors
of the Holocaust

by André Stein

> *Robert Krell is almost three years
> old when the Nazis occupy Holland.
> He soon loses the safety and security
> of his home and parents. He is
> taken into hiding. In his new
> environment, Robbie has to cope
> with anxiety, fear, and loneliness.*

A Matter of Joy: The Story of Robert Krell

Most families hiding Jewish children had a cover story for the child's sudden appearance in the community: he was a young cousin evacuated from Rotterdam after that city's massive bombing; she was a young niece needing shelter because her parents were temporarily unable to take care of her. The Munniks, however, chose to tell their three immediate neighbors the truth.

At first, they told everyone that Robbie was staying only a few weeks while his family searched for a permanent place for him. It's not that the Munniks were reckless; they just hadn't realized the full extent of the risk they were running by not keeping secret the fact that they had offered shelter to a Jewish child. As a matter of fact, they had never even given much thought to Jews one way or another. Robbie was probably the first Jew with whom they had contact. They had no use for or inclination towards hatred and persecution. Their attention was focused on living a simple existence. They worked; they took care of their small home; they communed with the members of their very large family. That was all.

Moeder and Vader, as Robbie called his rescuers, were kind people, and it took very little for him to learn to love them the way a small child loves his own mother and father. They were, indeed, fatherly and motherly in their solicitousness towards him. They even gave him their name. Thus he became Robbie Munnik. They also did their best to shelter the child from the harsh realities of the war. Moeder and Vader wanted him to have as normal a life as any child at that age. Yet, as much as Robbie loved Moeder and Vader, he never really forgot that they were not his real parents.

"All in all," recalls Dr. Robert Krell, today a professor of child psychiatry at the University of British Columbia in Vancouver, "I guess I had a wonderful existence. I can't imagine anyone having a better hiding experience than I did, because the Munniks were wonderful people. And while many others were hidden in closets, barns and dingy cellars, I had a terrific room to call my own."

One day, as Robbie was watching Violette Munnik prepare supper, he asked her what she was peeling.

"These are tulip bulbs," she answered. "They are for us. For you I have potatoes." But the boy knew better. He could tell that what he ate were not potatoes. Yet with the spontaneous generosity of the small child, Robbie colluded with them.

"The potatoes were great," he complimented Moeder.

The Munniks' daughter, Nora, was delighted with her brand-new brother. She felt important when she took care of him, played with him and taught him new things. "Nora was a wonderful teacher," Robert Krell recalls. "If it hadn't been for her, I'd have been a very lonely and ignorant child." She spent hours playing games with Robbie. Among other things, she taught him to read and write. And all this with patience that was exemplary for an adolescent.

Albert Munnik, in his quiet way, also took care of many of the young boy's needs. He spent his days working for the city's Department of Water Works. At night, he would bring home wood and busy himself with making toys for his new "son," who had arrived at his new home without any toys. Robbie's favorite was a wooden dog that moved its legs and wagged its tail, which he has to this day. And when he was finished making toys, Albert would sit Robbie on his lap and read to him. Or he would sit at the piano and play simple melodies he had taught himself. Indeed, he was a man of many talents, and he put all of them to the task of cheering up the little boy who had been forced to live in captivity without the company of friends.

Despite the Munniks' best efforts and the deepest affection, Robbie had a clear sense that there was danger in the air. Because of all the whispering, he concluded quite early in life that something menacing was happening. No one told him that the world outside had declared war on Jews, even on the children. Besides, he did not know what it meant to be Jewish. He sensed rather than knew that he was at risk. Did he do anything to earn the anger of these unknown forces? He was told that he was at the Munniks' because it was no longer safe for him to stay with his parents.

In the beginning, Emmy Krell managed to steal a few moments with her son. Leo also came to visit from time to time. On one occasion, he put his little boy on his lap and he taught him to call him Oom Leo (Uncle Leo). No reason was given for this change, thus increasing Robbie's fears. When children, especially the little ones, don't have tangible facts to account for their experience, they often sense danger.

Robbie's anxiety was further enhanced by his realization that his father was carrying a gun in his left inside jacket pocket. What did he need it for? Was he at risk? Every time he leaned against his father's chest, the boy knew something dangerous was in the air. "Many years later," Robert recalls, "while my father and I were reminiscing, I reminded him of the gun he was carrying in those days. My father denied the validity of my memory. If parents only had more respect for their young children's memories, they could learn a great deal about what the little ones really endured. Indeed, on further reflection, he conceded the correctness of my recollection: he had slipped the gun into the inside pocket of his jacket to make sure it would not get into my hands, as it was his habit to fling his jacket over a chair. Children do not forget unpleasant events or feelings. That gun in my dad's pocket was a source of anxiety for me. Hence, the gun's hard contour could never fade from the memory of my chest wall muscles."

And then, one day, about two months into Robbie's hiding, Uncle Leo stopped coming to visit. Curfews and random raids made it impossible for Leo to negotiate the streets of The Hague. The authorities had made the curfews ever more restrictive: if found outside after six o'clock, a Jew was shot on the spot. In addition, the German and Dutch raiding parties swept the streets with dogged thoroughness. Anyone caught was shipped to the transit camp at Westerbork, in the north-eastern province of Drenthe, and from there to Auschwitz, Mauthausen and, later, as the Eastern Front was moving west, to Bergen Belsen in Germany.

As for Robbie, he silently watched and waited. Unable to join the other children at play in the park across the street and too young to understand the reasons, he just did as he was told. All he knew was that he could not go out into the street because some horrible harm would come to him. "So I stayed in," recalls Robert Krell. "Since I was too young to have been used to an active social life in the world at large, it was more a vague curiosity about what was not available to me than a pining to be one of the people in the street. I was indeed very complacent, playing it very safe on every level."

Like thousands of other hidden children, especially the very young ones, Robbie remained quiet. He didn't have the words to ask the all-important questions, nor the intellectual arsenal to give voice to his secret bewilderment, or, for that matter, the courage to speak out. After all, just as these people had taken him in, they could send him away.

Like most hidden children, Robbie knew with a precocious, unspoken wisdom that his task was to be agreeable and silent. The best and the safest thing he could do was to go along with everything, not give his foster parents any trouble, and obey without questioning. Robbie was indeed compliant and happy to be so. He quickly realized that complaints and demands were out of the question. Who knew what they could lead to? Most children do not worry that they will be put out on the dangerous streets if they harangue their parents. But even with foster parents as wonderful as the Munniks, Robbie could not risk giving them a hard time or expressing preferences that could have rubbed them the wrong way. Indeed, silence was wisest. Thus, like most hidden children, Robbie learned the necessity of taming and befriending silence. As we shall see later, for many, silence turned into a "second wound" keeping them company for most of their lives, if not forever.

Unlike many hidden children, however, Robbie Krell seemed quite comfortable with his quiet solitude. But shortly after his arrival at the Munniks, his complacency was tested. One day, Vader, a resourceful man, proposed that Robbie watch him kill a rabbit he had brought home. By then, meat was a scarce commodity in most of the country.

The young boy was terrified at the very mention of killing an animal. He ran into the other room and hid. Robbie heard the thud of the bicycle pump used to bludgeon the animal. For the well-intentioned Dutchman, all this was a benign joke. Robbie, on the other hand, was repulsed at the thought of witnessing a slaughter. Albert did not insist.

Eventually, Robbie rose above his squeamishness and even took his share of the rabbit stew, plucking the bones clean – hunger prevailed over his natural revulsion – but he continued to feel that it was wrong to kill rabbits. The worst of it, however, for the three-year-old was that he did not feel free to discuss his sadness and his indignation with anyone. Would he have felt freer with his real parents? Probably. But instead he opted for being gracious and complacent – qualities that are scarcely typical for children at that age.

Violette Munnik's friends visited frequently, and to all of them she told the truth about her new young house guest.

A quiet conspiracy therefore followed to hide the boy's true identity from outsiders: what is amazing is that he was not betrayed. Robbie and the Munniks were most fortunate that the neighborhood wove a net of secrecy around them, safeguarding them from the authorities.

Kitty corner across the street from the Munniks lived Mr. de Vries, a well-known collaborator – one of some hundred thousand NSB-ers (members of the Dutch National Socialist Organization) who would have been only too happy to report to the authorities any suspicious individual. When, in 1961, Robert Krell returned to his native city, he knocked on the door of the Munniks' flat. Mr. de Vries opened his door first.

"Robbie?" the old man asked, not sure of his eyes. "Is that you?"

"Yes, Mr. de Vries, it's me."

"You know what?" he asked. "You never thanked me for not denouncing you to the authorities. I could have made big trouble for all of you, you know."

"You mean it actually occurred to you to betray me?" Rob asked incredulously, even though he knew betrayals were commonplace during the war.

How does one thank a person for not betraying him? Robert was stunned. Was he supposed to go around the streets of The Hague and shake the hands of all those who, like Mr. de Vries, didn't betray him and also cause the death of the Munnik family?

Although Robbie never went outside, everyone passing by the Munniks' place could see the child keeping a silent vigil by the window, a post he remained faithful to throughout nearly three years of hiding.

Nothing new ever happened outside, and yet it was worth watching – it was outside. Elsewhere Hitler waged war against Europe in general and against the Jews in particular. Battles were fought, bombs were dropped and Jews were deported to the killing fields in Germany and Eastern Europe. None of that was visible from the Munniks' window on Leonenschestraat in The Hague.

What the boy witnessed were the insignificant activities of everyday life in an occupied city street. He saw the same German soldiers in the park, horsing around like big boys, bullying one another and generally being rowdy. He had never seen anyone behave like them. He watched them urinate against the wall. In a more distant park, he saw misfired rockets land. Robbie observed the whole spectacle from his window.

In the fall of 1942, however, Violette and Albert noticed that the boy was becoming more and more downcast. They both knew that he suffered from being inside all the time. Although they received a lot of visitors, mostly members of their family, the boy was never allowed to pass beyond the threshold of their apartment. That, they decided, had to be the cause of his melancholy. He watched Nora go to school every day.

After carefully weighing the pros and cons, they decided it should be all right for Violette to take him with her shopping. What danger could they encounter? The next time Mrs. Munnik went to get her food ration coupons, she took with her an ecstatic little boy. A few blocks from their house, a total stranger came up to her.

"Isn't this little Robbie Krell?" the woman asked incredulously. "What are you doing with him? I know his mother."

Violette was stunned. This surprise encounter robbed her of her ability to speak. As she frantically scanned her brain for a plausible answer, the stranger, realizing how bewildered she was, came to her rescue.

"Not to worry, I'm a friend of the family. Your secret is buried with me. Here, you are likely to need this." The stranger handed Violette a ration card, flashed a smile at Robbie and disappeared around the corner.

The incident frightened the Munniks. Never again would they allow the boy to go out. He would just have to cope. Violette promised herself to do her best to chase the dark clouds of sadness from her little boy's eyes.

Somehow, with the special intuition of children, Nora sensed that her little "brother" needed some help. Without a word to anyone, she put the boy in a buggy. Although he was close to his third birthday, Robbie was not too big to fit into the deep carriage. She covered him with a blanket and told him to be nice and quiet. Then she set out towards her destination.

Nora had been wheeling the buggy for quite a while when they reached a viaduct, where she was forced to stop because the passage was flooded. One of the German soldiers standing guard came up. Hearing German spoken, the little boy barely allowed himself to breathe, and he pulled the covers over his head. The German soldier then picked up the buggy and carried it over the flooded section.

Forty years later, Robert Krell asked Nora where they had been headed on that adventurous outing. Nora refused to believe that he could remember any of it. "You were not even three years old," she insisted. "You couldn't remember any of it."

"I remember everything, Nora," Robert answered. "You put me in the buggy. You covered me with the blanket. And we went along the streets until that flooded viaduct. I remember the German, and I remember how scared I was, expecting to be discovered by him. Where were we going? Why did you take me out in spite of all the risks, in spite of your parents' decision to keep me in all the time?"

"Well," she answered, "I was twelve years old. You were a little kid, scarcely bigger than a baby. I figured you needed to see your mother. So I wanted to take you to her."

"Did we make it, Nora?"

"No, we turned around and went right back after the German soldier helped us. When we got home, I received the first and only spanking of my life. I never took you out again."

Life continued along an uneventful path for the boy. Except for the great famine during the exceptionally cold winter of 1945, little disturbed his life. By then, more than two and a half years had passed since he had gone into hiding. He had not seen his mother or father for almost that long. For a while his elusive "uncle" would come and put him on his lap and tell him stories. But those memories evaporated into the thin air of youthful oblivion. Little by little, all his memories of life before his arrival at the Munniks' receded. As far as he was concerned, Albert and Violette were his mother and father.

Then one day in May 1945, an extraordinary thing happened. The adults around Robbie were all laughing and crying. Strangers embraced and sang together. Perched at his look-out, Robbie saw the street come alive. A most extraordinary spectacle, indeed. And no one told him to step back lest someone might see him.

On the contrary, Violette and Albert, in spite of their habitual reserve, hugged the confused little boy and told him over and over that from now on he was going to be free.

The Munniks took Robbie on the flat roof of their building where, together with other residents, they watched as the British Air Force took possession of the sky. Everyone pointed at large parcels that floated on parachutes towards the ground. The British were dropping loads of white bread over Holland. That finally convinced Robbie that, indeed, liberation had to be a happy event.

A few days after liberation, a couple showed up at the Munniks' door. Robbie did not know who they were, although they looked vaguely familiar.

After a couple of minutes of whispering with the Munniks, the strangers came over to Robbie. Moeder and Vader stood behind them without a word. The woman reached out to hug Robbie, and the man put a trembling hand on his shoulder. The boy recoiled from them. At age five, he was no longer in the habit of being intimate with total strangers.

"Robbie darling," the woman said in a gentle but shaky voice, "do you remember us? I am your mother, and this is your father."

The boy didn't believe his ears. What did this woman mean? His parents were standing right behind the strangers. And how was it that Moeder and Vader were willing to go along with this nonsense? Why didn't they ask these strangers to leave?

Robbie moved back a few more steps. With his eyes he implored the Munniks to come to his aid. They both looked pale and sad.

"You are not my parents!" he shouted at the couple. "Moeder, Vader, tell them that you are my parents and to leave me alone."

Moeder silently nodded. For the first time, Robbie saw tears in her eyes. Then he noticed that the woman who claimed to be his mother was also weeping silently.

Robbie made a dash for Albert Munnik and threw himself against his vader.

"How can I convince you that you are our little boy?" Emmy asked through her tears. "We had to leave you with the Munniks. Believe me, we had to. And they took very good care of you and you love them and they love you. But now it is time to start living again as a family. Come, my darling. Come to your mother."

The boy held on to Albert's pants even tighter. None of this made any sense to him.

But what else could they have told him? That they were Jews and the Germans came and tried to kill them so they all had to go into hiding? That they gave him away, but now they wanted him back because somehow it all worked out? All that would have just further confused the bewildered child. How could they have explained what had pitted adult against adult, when the realities made no sense even to the parents? What are Jews? What is hiding? Is hiding living with the Munniks for as long as he could remember? Is it staying inside all the time? What's wrong with being inside when you don't know what is outside?

"Don't you remember me, Robbie?" Leo tried his luck. "I used to visit you a couple of years ago. I never said I was your father, though. I pretended to be your uncle Leo, just to make it easier for you. You would sit on my lap and I'd tell you stories."

Now that this man came forward and spoke to Robbie, a whisper of memory returned. Yes, he recalled Uncle Leo. Yes, he did like to sit on his lap and listen to his stories.

"So what if you're my uncle Leo?" Robbie asked defiantly. "That doesn't prove you're my parents. I want to stay with Moeder and Vader. Please let me be. This isn't fair."

The four adults looked at each other. They agreed with the boy; it was not fair to expect him to leave the only parents he knew. They had to take another approach.

The next day the Krells came back with an album full of photos of Robbie with Emmy and Leo in their home on Suez Street. At first the boy only glanced at the pictures. But after he saw a few of them, his heart sank. He recognized himself as a toddler surrounded by these people. There was not one picture of him and the Munniks.

"So what if I used to be your kid?" He continued to struggle for his cause. "You left me and now I'm Robbie Munnik. I'm not going with you. I'm not going with you anywhere."

He was screaming uncontrollably. Violette Munnik wanted to put her arms around her little boy, but she realized that now it was Emmy Krell's turn to mother "their" boy.

A little later, the Krells left the Munniks' apartment with their heavy-hearted son. Leo carried him down the stairs, while Albert gave a hand with his bagful of clothes and toys.

"You come and visit us, my boy, you hear?" Albert said as he waved goodbye. "Our door is always open to you.

But for now have a good life with your wonderful parents."

Robbie whimpered all the way to his new home.

Little by little he learned to love the Krells again, who, in turn encouraged him to continue to love the Munniks, too. Although he was allowed to pay frequent visits to his moeder and vader, he missed his daily life with them. That sadness has never left Robbie. To this day, when he thinks of the Munniks, his eyes cloud over.

HIDE ME, BUBBA CHAYE

Translated from the Yiddish by Seymour Levitan

by Rachel Korn

Hide me, Bubba Chaye, hold me,
eldest daughter of your youngest son
your only living grandchild,
spread your apron out again and take me in.

Where I am
dickering tongues waver
on scales with nothing to weigh,
and the late autumn blows into
my unsecured day.

Wait for me on the clay hill
by twisting foxholes,
till I run home from school again
breathless and scared to death.

Button my undone hour
like my coat, to keep me from freezing,
and quickly so no one hears
unsay the evil eye from my overheated brow –
who can say the words as well as you?

Then lay your hands on my eyes
and help me see better
how to go home.

CHILD OF THE HOLOCAUST

by Jack Kuper

In the Polish countryside, eight-year-old Jacob is separated from his parents. He lives with a strange woman, who makes him work hard for his food and shelter. His greatest wish is to find his home and parents.

Chapter One

A heavy layer of mist covered the village of Kulik, disclosing a few chimneys and thatch roofs as if they were suspended in the air.

I sat in the back of the wagon, clutching the bag of food in my hands, and listened to the wheels turning and the horse's trot.

Mrs. Paizak sat in the front holding the reins, her back towards me. "Vio!" she called out to the horse whenever he slowed down, and hit him across the back.

The horse too could barely be seen, and it seemed as if we were sitting on a cloud being pulled by some magic force.

Perhaps all this is a dream I thought. When I wake I'll find Mrs. Paizak and Genia gone.

Every week on market day Mrs. Paizak drove into Siedliszcze. She would sell some produce, buy a dress or pair of shoes, matches, oil, or a reel of thread. Usually Genia would accompany her and I'd be left behind to feed the pigs and the chickens, take care of the cows, and wait impatiently for their return with messages from my mother.

For the first time since leaving home I was now going to see my mother. There are so many things I want to tell her. How exciting! She'll be so surprised – she probably doesn't even expect me! What will she say when I hand her the bundle and she opens it and discovers a loaf of bread, some potatoes, a small bag of flour and three eggs?

I pressed this treasure against my body and could see my mother's dark eyes beaming with pride.

The same eyes several weeks earlier had covered my cheeks with tears. "He's only a child, Mrs. Paizak. How can I let him go?"

"I'm not a child any more," I answered indignantly. "I'm nine!"

"You're eight, Jankele," my mother smiled. I lowered my head.

"Well, I'm almost nine, and please don't call me Jankele, my name is Jakob."

The mist settled, and a slow-rising sun appeared. The countryside now visible was moving away from me – mud houses with small windows and crooked chimneys from which black smoke rose, here and there a cowhand taking his herd to pasture, a cock waking the village.

In a meadow an old farmer was ploughing. By the road-side an angry dog barked, and over the road hung a huge dead tree. Under this tree lay a stone on a crudely made grave and buried in the cold ground beneath was my grandfather; but for a moment I now imagined he was running behind our wagon, dressed in his brown leather coat and hat with earflaps. Icicles hung from his nostrils and beard, and his worn black boots were caked with snow. With the one hand he held the burlap bag, which hung over his right shoulder, with the other he stretched towards me and called out, "Jankele, wait! I need a ride into town."

Several times Mrs. Paizak turned to look at me and once she patted the top of my head and winked. I smiled and in a soft voice began to sing a song about an orphaned shepherd boy named Franek:

Franek takes his cows to pasture,
And on his flute he plays,
But what sad forlorn tones
Drift, drift across the countryside.

We now crossed the wooden bridge over the River Wieprz and were soon driving through winding narrow streets. It was unnaturally quiet. There was not a living creature to be seen, except a cat roaming the rooftops. Broken household articles littered the roads. Suddenly through the streets echoed the horrible sound of uncontrolled laughter.

I stared from side to side, then turned to look at Mrs. Paizak. She was staring at me but quickly turned and faced the horse, lashed him across the back and shouted, "Vio!" The horse began to gallop, the wagon jumped and shook along the cobbled road then came to a sudden halt in the market place.

The stalls were not there, the square was deserted and loose pillow feathers hung in the air like snowflakes in the winter. Across the square a band of peasants came out of a house carrying a chest of drawers. Another carried a mattress, and a young woman was trying on a coat and circling like a ballerina. An aged man, bent in half and carrying a tailor's dummy, suddenly appeared in front of us.

"Where is everyone?" asked Mrs. Paizak.

The old man's eyes slowly widened, he set the dummy down and then answered, "Last night, in the middle of the night, the Germans came and took all the Jews away. They marched them out like a herd of cattle. There isn't one left!"

"Dear Jesus!" exclaimed Mrs. Paizak and made the sign of the cross.

I stared at the man, unable to move or say anything, then suddenly I jumped off the wagon and began to run. My feet pounded the cobbled road and carried me faster than I had ever imagined possible. The houses seemed to be removed from their foundations and reclined at different angles; sometimes they appeared to sway from one side to the other and even turn upside-down. Soon they were no more than fast-moving blurs passing in front of my eyes.

Mrs. Paizak, I've left Mrs. Paizak. Why am I even thinking about Mrs. Paizak? But what if she needs my assistance? What about Genia? Has she taken the cows to pasture? Why do I persist in thinking about these things?

I finally came to a halt and now the small crooked window of my home was before me. I had hoped to see my little brother Josele's face in it and hear him shout, "Mama, Mama,

Jankele is home!" But the glass was now shattered and no one looked out from behind the pane.

Isn't it possible, I began to think, that by some miracle, by some fortunate chance, by an act of God, my family is still inside? Perhaps they hid in the attic, or in the cellar, or under the bed, or maybe the Germans who came to get them took pity and spared them! It's possible. Why not?

The door lay broken on the veranda, torn from its hinges. That's only for appearance, I consoled myself, to make it seem that no one lives there. It's possible, in fact it's very clever.

I entered. A few pots stood on the stove. A torn straw mattress lay on the floor, a sheet beside it. Several of the floor-boards had been removed and in the corner, crumpled and dirty, lay a small drawing of Tarzan swinging from a tree.

Uncle Shepsel, I thought. Will I ever see him make draw-ings of Tarzan again? Will I ever hear his voice keeping me spellbound for hours with tales about cowboys and Indians in a distant strange land?

"Mama!" I whispered. "Josele, Shepsel . . . don't be afraid, it's safe to come out now."

At my feet lay two small pieces of fur, which I immediately recognized as having once adorned my mother's coat pockets. I picked them up and once more called:

"Josele! Shepsel! Mama! Please come out, it's Jankele."

I must cry. Why can't I cry? I'll think of onions, or the little bird I treasured once then found dead, its head crushed between two bars at the cage. I cried then, why can't I cry now? I must cry. What else can I think of? Quickly something unpleasant has to come to my mind. . . .

Suddenly I heard footsteps.

Perhaps it's my mother! It's possible, why not? No, it's probably a German coming to get me. I'll hide . . . but where? No, why hide? I want to be taken with the others. I'll go willingly.

I faced the door. Mrs. Paizak's stocky figure appeared. Her eyes were wet, her head tilted to one side. She made several attempts to say something but nothing came out. She scanned the room, examining the few articles there and finally said, "Jakob, we might as well take these." I remained silent. "If we don't some strangers will grab them," and she gathered the articles into the sheet.

She asked about the pieces of fur in my hands but I refused to part with them and stuffed them into my pocket.

"My mother will be worried about me," I finally said.

"She knows you're in good hands my child," answered Mrs. Paizak tying the sheet.

"How will I be able to live alone?" She fell to her knees, held my face in the palms of her hands and said:

"You won't be alone. I'll look after you."

"But there's no one left from my family."

"What about your Uncle Moishe?" she asked. "Isn't he working in some village?"

My Uncle Moishe! How can I find him? Perhaps he was at home visiting and was also taken away. How can I find out? Where can I look for him? I have to find him.

My arm was suddenly pulled and I found myself outside. The looters were now to be seen everywhere, carrying axes and saws, shouting and laughing and fighting for the spoils.

Outside town more of them with empty burlap bags under their arms were walking briskly towards Siedliszcze and as they passed us they shouted, "Anything left there, or did you grab everything?"

Again I saw the tree, the grave, the stone, and once more my grandfather, Shie Chuen the shoemaker, from Pawia Street in Warsaw, was trudging along the snow-covered road.

Suddenly, out of the blinding snowstorm, came three German soldiers on horseback, their faces covered in shadow. One soldier drew his revolver and fired. My grandfather only wavered. The second German aimed. A bullet whistled through the air and found its target. The shoemaker groaned, but still stood. The third bullet was the fatal one. The massive old man in the brown leather coat fell to the ground. The burlap bag flew through the air and out of it fell pieces of bread, frozen potatoes and shoemaker's tools.

"Have mercy," he whispered and his lips closed forever.

"Say something, Kubush," I suddenly heard Mrs. Paizak say.

"Kubush? My name isn't Kubush."

"It's the same as Jakob," she answered, "only more fitting for a little boy like you."

I turned my back to her and in choking tones began to sing:

Kubush takes his cows to pasture,
And on his flute he plays,
But what sad forlorn tones
Drift, drift across the countryside.

Why such sad melody poor orphan boy
Do you play on your flute?
Perhaps the world is mistreating you,
Tell me, tell it to . . .

And then the tears came, and I began to sob.

"Poor boy, poor boy," I heard Mrs. Paizak mutter to herself. The tears filled my eyes and blinded my vision.

The road, the little houses with the straw roofs, seemed to melt.

THE SECRET OF GABI'S DRESSER

by Kathy Kacer

> *Nazi troops invade Czechoslovakia.*
> *Jewish girls face deportation. Gabi's*
> *mother warns her daughter to*
> *practise hiding in readiness for the*
> *day the soldiers come to their door.*
> *The only place possible is dark,*
> *cramped, and airless. Panic over-*
> *whelms Gabi. How will she endure?*

Chapter Twelve
April 1943

The second chance to practise never came. In fact, crazy as it sounds, months went by and we almost forgot about me hiding in the dresser. The news about raids and people being taken away pretty much stopped during this time. Apparently, local people and government officials had started to complain about the disappearance of Jewish doctors, lawyers and business people. In the face of these complaints, the campaign of perse-cution slowed down for a period of time. That's not to say that the restrictions and discrimination ended. We were still not allowed to go to school, food was still hard to come by and looting was still a regular occurrence.

Occasionally, Mamma would say I should practise hiding in the dresser again. She even suggested having someone come over to see if there was a way to create air holes in the back, so I could breathe better inside. But every time she mentioned anything like that, I managed to distract her and change the topic. It was almost as if we had convinced ourselves that the problems were over and that life would soon return to normal. In fact, our lives did slip into a kind of routine, in spite of everything happening around us. So it came as an even bigger shock when the nightmare suddenly arrived.

I was alone at home, playing with the kitten in the front yard. Mamma had gone to Marishka's house to see if she could find any clothing for us. Marishka's family had left a week earlier, taking only enough clothes and belongings to make the journey overseas to America. They had left everything else behind.

It had taken them a long time to gather the necessary travel papers. The longer Marishka remained in our village, the more I tried to convince myself that she might not go. But finally the day had come for her departure. I tried telling her that her family was crazy to leave. But who was I to think I could change her mind? In the end, we vowed that somehow we would see each other again in the future.

Before saying goodbye, Marishka's mother had made us promise to go through the house and take whatever we needed. Mamma had left early in the morning and, though she always worried when she left me alone, I had assured her that I would be fine.

The kitten was chasing butterflies as usual, and I laughed each time she leapt in the air, trying in vain to capture just one unsuspecting creature. I was so involved in my play that I barely heard Mamma's voice calling in the distance.

"Gabi! The soldiers! The trucks! They're coming now! Run and hide!" I turned to see Mamma rushing up the path to the house, fear and panic etched in her face. At first I didn't understand what she was saying. Was this a joke? Was she pretending so that I would be forced to practise hiding again? Then I thought that maybe she had hurt herself, or something had happened to someone else. As she reached the house and shouted again, I realized that this was the real thing. The danger we had been dreading was on our doorstep.

"Gabi! No time to lose. You must hide in the dresser."

The full impact of what she was saying began to sink in, and for a moment I couldn't move. I felt as if my legs were glued to the ground, and I thought crazily that the soldiers were going to find me there, stuck, unable to get away. I shook my head in a daze. Hide, I thought. I've got to hide. I reached for the kitten, but Mamma pulled my arms away.

"No, Gabi. There's no time for the kitten. Leave her here." She grabbed my hand and yanked me towards the house. Together we headed for the dining room and ran to the dresser. Mamma got there first and opened the door, motioning me to climb inside. I hesitated for a moment, peering into the darkness, remembering the disastrous practice a few months earlier.

My first thought was that I couldn't do it. My body stiffened as I remembered how dark and cramped the dresser had been. Beads of sweat broke out on my forehead and upper lip as I recalled how hot and crushed I had felt. Shaking with fear, I wondered if I was going to faint. How could I possibly climb inside the dresser and stay there?

But I had no choice. This was my only chance for safety. At any minute the soldiers would burst through the door, and once they arrived, there would be no hope for me. I was certain to be taken away. My choice was to face the soldiers or face the darkness.

"Hurry, hurry!" Mamma shouted again. "Inside, and not a sound." I had never seen her so frightened. Taking a deep breath, I bent my head and crawled into the dresser. As I settled into the darkness, Mamma quickly closed the door behind me. I heard the sound of the key turning in the lock. I shut my eyes tightly, held my breath and tried to control the rapid beating of my heart.

The dresser felt even worse than the last time. Why hadn't we thought of putting a pillow in here, or something else soft for me to hold onto? There was nothing here except wood and nails. I hugged my body for comfort, but it wasn't enough. I thought to myself, if I scream, Mamma will come and get me. She'll open the door and hold me. I needed air but there wasn't any. Maybe if I opened the door for just a minute, and took a deep breath and then closed the door again, I would feel better. What was I thinking of? This jumble of thoughts was crazy. I knew I couldn't do anything. The soldiers were coming and I had to stay put.

It wasn't long before I heard a muffled pounding at the front door of our house. Harsh, deep voices were talking but I couldn't make out the words. Occasionally the voices grew louder, mixed with the sound of Mamma saying something I couldn't understand. I thought I heard someone say "girl" and then "search," but I couldn't be sure. It sounded as if a lot of people were in the house. I could hear cupboard doors opening and closing. Every now and then I thought I heard a crash, as if something had broken.

My eyes were still closed, my ears straining to make sense of the sounds outside. My heart was beating so loud and fast that I thought it was going to come right out through my chest. What if someone outside heard? My breathing was quick and shallow as I gulped in tiny mouthfuls of air. I knew that if I didn't slow down my breathing, I was in danger of passing out. Sweat was pouring from my upper lip and forehead. I've got to relax, I thought hopelessly, as I buried my head deep in my chest.

I was frantically worried about Mamma and her safety. What would the soldiers do if they didn't find me? Would they take her instead? Would they hurt her? Then, as I heard voices moving closer to the dresser, I panicked and thought they had found me. What would the soldiers do once they got their hands on me? I knew I would be taken away, but where? Would I be harmed? Would I ever see Mamma again? Each minute felt like a lifetime. It was unbearable to be inside the dresser, and even more unbearable not to know what was happening outside. I hugged my knees closer to my chest and prayed this ordeal would end soon.

Suddenly, I heard something at the door of the dresser. What was that noise? It sounded like sandpaper rubbing against the wood, or some kind of scratching. The soldiers hadn't left yet, so I knew it wasn't Mamma coming to free me. Was it a soldier? Had I been discovered? Maybe Mamma had been right after all, the dresser was too obvious a place to hide. I waited a moment, thinking the door would open, but it didn't. Yet the scratching continued. And then I heard a faint mew and I knew what it was. Mashka! The kitten must have seen me crawl into the dresser, and now she was coming to sniff me out!

For one second I forgot my panic and nearly laughed out loud at the craziness of it all. Here I was, thinking that soldiers were about to break into the dresser to find me, when in fact my own little kitten was about to betray me, by scratching and mewing at the door. What a ridiculous way to be discovered!

The moment of humor didn't last long. Within seconds, the sound of Mashka's scratching was replaced by the clumping of boots moving closer and closer. Now I knew my time was up. At any moment they would demand that Mamma open the dresser door. The wave of panic returned full force, and I clenched my fists to my face, biting hard on my hand to stop from screaming out loud. I closed my eyes again and prayed silently for my safety.

And then, in the darkness of my hiding place, I became aware of something close to me. At first I felt something warm, as if strong arms were reaching out to surround me. I opened my eyes and peered into the murky shadows. I couldn't see a thing, but I still felt something there. As I turned my head to the left and right I sensed it again and again. I couldn't quite describe the feeling. Was it a smell? Like shaving lotion? No, perhaps the faint odor of a pipe. It was achingly familiar, and it filled the corners of the dresser until I finally realized what it was. Papa! His smell, his smile. Outside the dresser, the shuffling and pounding of the soldiers' search continued. But inside the dresser I felt the warmth of Papa's gaze on my face, and slowly I felt my body begin to relax. The rapid beating of my heart slowed down. My breathing became quieter and more even. My fears began to disappear. It was as if Papa were there with me, to protect me as he had done when he was alive. I heard him speak, and I listened to his comforting voice:

I will shelter you from harm,
You must have no fear,
You'll be safe, my precious child,
You'll be safe, my dear.

Over and over I heard Papa's voice repeating the poem. And each time I heard the poem, and each time I saw Papa's smile, I felt myself grow calmer and calmer. The voices outside the dresser were now just a muffled hum in the distance. The darkness around me no longer felt cold. The wooden floor of the dresser seemed to cushion me. I felt warm and protected. I knew I would be safe.

II

Loss and Exile

SURVIVOR STORY:
I Chose

by Marion Kaufmann Cassirer

I was born in Berlin in 1936, where I lived with my parents until 1942, when my father was arrested by the Nazis. We never saw him again. Mother and I fled to Holland and were hidden by the members of the underground. Once, when on my way to have my hair bleached, I was arrested, but the "underground" rescued me. I was placed with a wonderful Catholic family who lived near Arnhem. We were liberated by the Canadians in September 1944, and a year later my mother and I were reunited. I did not remember her, even though it had only been three years since we had been separated.

"Choose," she said, rather impatiently, "I have to complete this form to register you for school."

"Choose," I thought, "I just had my ninth birthday and I'm supposed to make a decision that will affect me the rest of my life." Actually I thought I was only eight, because I was very small and had been told again and again: "You are five, remember you are five." Fives were good, sixes were bad. As we started our escape, fives were safe; sixes had to wear the yellow star. No wonder I only remembered the day but not the age I really was. It was just one more addition to the stone necklace that was pulling my life down.

My mother had changed everything since she first appeared at the farmhouse where I was hidden barely three months ago. This old-looking woman, with the missing teeth, straggly hair, funny accent and flabby white skin. Everyone said this was really my mother and I had to call her Mama. This perfect stranger? How could *she* be my mother? I had a family already.

She brought me here to Amsterdam and nothing was the same. I could not cross myself and pray on my knees in front of my bed at night. I could not go to church. I could not have milk with my dinner, I could not – I could not. I had to be Jewish, whatever that was. Praying I understood, the language I didn't. She took me away from all I knew and loved. *That* me was no more.

"Well," she interrupted my musings, "which is it going to be?" The choice was easy after all. Renie was left behind, the new me would continue on.

"Marion," I said, "I am Marion."

Who and what would I be today if I had chosen Renie?

SURVIVOR STATEMENT

MARGOT HOWELL

My name is Margot Howell. I was twelve years old when I had to leave my parents in Vienna in 1939.

Being the only child, it was especially hard for all of us to part.

I had never been away from my parents. My journey to England by *Kindertransport* was very emotional.

I never saw my parents again.

I had nothing. My only memento was a blue pincushion my mother had made from the remnant of an old dirndl skirt.

After meeting my foster parents, my life changed completely. I had to grow up quickly. My foster parents were not of the nurturing kind.

My new life involved being brought up in a Christian household and going to a Catholic school.

I did not want to be Jewish anymore, I just wanted to belong somewhere.

Then the war came and I had to leave school at fourteen at my foster parents' request. I went to work and lost out on being a teenager.

It took me a long time before I could face being Jewish again.

SURVIVOR STORY:

In a Time of Terror:
When Will Mother
Return?

by René Goldman

I was born in 1934 in Luxembourg, the capital city of the grand Duchy of Luxembourg, a small country of about 400,000 inhabitants squeezed between France, Belgium, and Germany. The official language of the country is French, but the people also speak German and a German dialect called *Lëtzebuergesch*.

Luxembourg was a carefree happy little country, before the war. I can imagine how anguished my parents must have felt when, from only a few kilometers away, echoes reached them of the hate-filled bark resounding from the throat of a murderous lunatic frothing at the mouth, and millions of Germans roaring with him, "*Sieg heil!*" and "Death to the Jews!"

One Sunday morning my father and I, while walking past the railway station, saw columns of marching German soldiers. Luxembourg, like Belgium and Holland, was now occupied. Harassment soon began of the 5000 Jewish people, followed by arrests and deportations. My parents and I moved to the Belgian capital, Brussels, a large city where we hoped to live unnoticed.

The year was 1942 and I was eight years old. Jews were compelled to wear a yellow star stamped with the letter J sewn on their clothes. One afternoon in a cinema when I took off my coat, the star was revealed. The children around me booed and mocked me, shouting, "*Juif! Juif!*" I ran home in tears and declared to my parents that I was not going to wear that star any longer. Failing to reason with me, my parents decided not to wear the star either, regardless of the danger. Signs "Jews and dogs not admitted" now went up in front of the cinemas and other public places.

A month later, mighty France, the largest country of Europe, was in her turn occupied by German forces. Democracy collapsed, Marshal Pétain became dictator and accepted the partition of France into two zones: an Occupied Zone in the North, which included Paris, and a Non-Occupied or Free Zone in the South. Gradually all avenues of escape from Europe were closed.

That summer we left Brussels and all our possessions and fled across the border to France. With a group of friends we managed to cross the Occupied Zone, traveling by train, by bus, on foot, even on bicycle, until we reached the Demarcation Line, which separated the Occupied Zone from the Free Zone. In a small village near the Swiss border we were met by a guide, who took us across the line. We had to crawl through fields of hops, then walk through woods, hiding now and then in ditches, until the guide motioned us on. Having marched the whole night long made me marvel at my own stamina. My parents hoped to cross Southern France, reach Marseille, and there catch a boat bound for Uruguay. In the dark of night, huddled in a ditch in the forest, my father whispered to me about a beautiful city called Montevideo, where, if we were lucky, we would soon live. . . .

But luck did not smile on us. At dawn, as we walked out of the forest into the Non-Occupied Zone, we were caught by the French police. They took us by train to the town of Lons-le-Saunier, where we were assigned to stay at a small requisitioned hotel with other Jews caught when they clandestinely crossed the Demarcation Line. We could walk freely about the town, but were not allowed to travel outside of it.

Mother wrote to her older sister, Aunt Fella, who lived with her family in Limoges. Being French citizens, they were not yet in any danger; furthermore, my cousin Simon, twenty years older than me, was a lieutenant in the French army and had in 1940 defended the city of Vichy, to which the French government had moved from Paris. Mother wanted Aunt Fella to come and take me away to live with her and Uncle David.

Then came that awful morning. Shortly before 8:00 a.m., Mother, visibly shaken, woke me up with the frightening news that policemen were waiting for us in front of the hotel, and that I should dress quickly and go down with her. Father luckily had gone out to buy a newspaper. The policemen in black uniforms had come to arrest a number of us, Jewish refugees from Belgium, Holland, and Luxembourg. They marched us through the town: a lugubrious procession of frightened men, women, and children. Commanding this operation against helpless people was a brutal commissar with a thick mustache, who hurried us on with shoves and shouts like "Move on, you dirty Jews!"

Mother was in tears and prompted me to cry, as if this could soften the stone hearts of our escorts. In this hour of tragedy I felt too numb to cry. Soon we stopped in front of the small railway station. By a miraculous coincidence, at that very moment Aunt Fella arrived on a train from distant Limoges. She saw us as she walked out of the station and, with a shocked look on her face, cried: *"Mon Dieu, quel malheur!"* (My God, what misfortune!) Then, in a blinking of an eye, while the commissar's back was turned, she seized me by the hand and pulled me away, whispering energetically: *"Viens, sauve-toi avec moi!"* (Come, run away with me!) But in my state of shock I could not run.

Running would, in any case, have been futile as the commissar turned around, saw us, and rushed after us. Seizing my aunt, who was a tiny woman of fifty, by the collar of her coat, he violently slapped her. Then he grabbed me by the hair and the seat of my trousers and, tugging at my hair till I screamed, ran to throw me into the train, into which my unfortunate companions were being hurled in an indescribable atmosphere of chaos and terror. In that terrifying instant I saw policemen dragging my mother, who was kicking and screaming, over the floor of the station. Just as that black-uniformed brute held me in front of the train, a miracle happened. Two gendarmes in khaki uniforms appeared on the platform and said something to the commissar, who, without a word, handed me over to them. They were kind; one of them with a protective hand turned my head against his chest, so that I would see no more of what was happening. Then, after a few minutes, he gently let go and said: "Now you may look: your mother is leaning out of that window over there, waving to you. . . ." As I waved back to her the train moved. That was the last time I saw my mother. . . .

After the train carrying my mother left, the khaki-uniformed gendarmes returned me to Aunt Fella, who took me to the home of people she knew. In the afternoon I was taken to see my father, who had gone into hiding. We wept bitterly together.

Several days later, Aunt Fella took me with her to Limoges. Not long after my visit in Lyon, Father came to live there with Uncle Paul and his family. I lived a short time with Aunt Fella and Uncle David Domb and their children, as French citizens living in the Free Zone. Soon an unknown woman took me by train to the Creuse, a region of central France, where many Jewish children were sheltered in a group of castles run by the OSE, a children's aid society.

The place I was brought to was the Chateau de Masgelier. It was a castle of awesome appearance. Being an only child who had been pampered by my parents, I was terrified of being made to live in such a large collective of total strangers. To sleep with many other boys in a dormitory room, be wakened in the morning by a woman who barged in brusquely, forced us to dress and wash in a hurry, and then march to the castle for breakfast and the day's activities, was more than I could bear at a time when I felt desperately lonely. I wrote pleading letters to Aunt Fella to come and take me away from Masgelier. My pleadings brought forth fruit. A couple of weeks after I arrived there, again a lady came for me. Had I remained at Masgelier, I would once more have fallen into the clutches of those who wanted me dead.

My chaperone was one of those young women, Jewish and Christian, some of them social workers, who volunteered for the dangerous task of escorting Jewish children to places of hiding. The woman did not take me back to Limoges: instead, she accompanied me and a dozen other boys and girls to a village called Vendoeuvres, some fifty kilometers from Chateauroux. There I spent the winter of 1942–43: first with a family called Lamoureux in Vendoeuvres proper, then with the more congenial Cassaud family – a young couple with a baby, who lived in a single-room hut several kilometers from the village.

Life in Vendoeuvres was peaceful, almost happy. I was not aware that on November 11, the Germans had invaded the South and that there no longer was a Non-Occupied Zone.

One midmorning in February, I sat in class as usual when my host father, Jean Cassaud, walked in and spoke to our teacher, Monsieur Renard. I said goodbye to my classmates and Jean Cassaud took me home for lunch, then back to the village, to the railway station, all the while telling me that I was going to travel to Lyon to be reunited with my father. I was, naturally, overjoyed, as I missed Father and Mother so badly. What a surprise awaited me in front of the station: standing there, with a strange man and woman, were all the Jewish children hidden in Vendoeuvres! Soon we were aboard a train that was traveling west, which intrigued me, since Lyon, some 800 kilometers away, was in the direction of the southeast. I queried our chaperones and the man whispered to me that I was indeed not going to Lyon, that they were taking us somewhere where no one could find us!

At the station in Buzancais, we had to change trains: the lady took the girls on one train, and the man took the boys on another train. Around midnight we were brought to a Roman Catholic convent school called Les Besses. The nuns, who had been waiting up for the four of us, gave us new identities, which we were made to commit to memory before being sent to bed. I thus became René Gamier, supposedly born in Chateauroux. We were warned never to tell any of the French boys who we were.

I spent fifteen months, which seemed like an eternity, at Les Besses. The convent stood on a remote hilltop; the nearest town, kilometers away, was Pellevoisin, celebrated for its appearance of the Virgin Mary years before. In its drab and drafty halls I felt cold, hungry, and forlorn. Every day, we ate rutabagas and turnips and little else. The nuns were protective of us, the four Jewish boys. Every Sunday a priest came to celebrate mass in the chapel, and the nuns so arranged the schedule that none of us ever served as altar boy, even though I very much wanted to. But we had to attend chapel service morning and evening, recite prayers before and after meals, before and after class, and at bedtime.

Never before did time pass so slowly as it did at Les Besses. It was therefore with real trepidation that one afternoon, at the end of April 1944, I beheld a stranger walking up the alley in the woods that led to the school: it was a lady come to take me away. This time it was truly to Lyon that I traveled! My cousin Ginette met me at the station. No words can describe the joy that exploded in me when, in the single-room flat on the top floor of an old slum, I beheld Father, seated with Uncle Paul and Aunt Zilly.

I spent several weeks in Lyon. Father worked, under a false identity, in a tailoring workshop. At night much of his time was taken up by his secret work in the Jewish underground resistance movement. He always tried to come home to tuck me in, but sometimes danger forced him to sleep elsewhere. Whenever he sat by my bedside, I would grill him with questions, such as: when will the Allies land? When will that terrible war end? When will Mother return? Will I have a little sister after the war, as they had promised?

On June 6, 1944, I heard on the radio that the Allied armies had landed in Normandy. I was so excited that I ran down to the workshop to announce the news to Father and his workmates. The boss treated us all to a drink at a nearby café – wine for the men and grape juice for me.

Meanwhile the ferocity of the German occupiers seemed to increase in proportion to the progress made by the Allied armies. Air raids became more frequent, but even as bombs rained over the city, we hesitated to go into the underground shelters for fear that someone might recognize us and report us. Father took me then to Chozeau, a village between Lyon and Grenoble, where he hid with a farming family for the summer.

Lyon was liberated in September and soon Aunt Zilly came to bring me home with her. Not wanting to cause me more grief, she told me that Father had enrolled in the Free French Forces at the time of the Liberation. Going to school again, I felt intensely proud that my father was a soldier and that he would return a hero after the war. That winter after the liberation of Lyon was a bitterly cold and hungry one, but at last we could breathe!

Aunt Zilly, who had three children of her own to feed, sent me away to a Jewish children's group home in Bourg d'Oisans, in the Alps. That is where the end of the war found me on that unforgettable day of May 8, 1945. But the hope that blossomed in my heart that spring slowly withered as days, weeks, months went by, with no sign that my parents would ever return. It was then that I learned of the terrible fate of six million of my fellow Jews.

Beginning in the summer of 1945, I grew up in a succession of children's homes near Paris. During the day I was absorbed by school, play, and other activities. But at night I saw my parents in dreams and often cried under my sheets. Every now and then an adult would arrive at the home: someone's mother or father had returned, and as that kid burst with joy, my heart would sink further, for in the end no one ever came for me. I learned very soon that Mother had been murdered in Auschwitz, but I long deluded myself that Father might still reappear. It was not until two years after the war that a visitor from Lyon told me the truth that my aunt and uncle had hidden from me: namely, that Father had been caught one month before the liberation of Lyon and that he was on the last train that left France for Auschwitz. He collapsed at the end of a death march, a mere six weeks before the end of the war.

More than half a century has gone by since those sad years of my early childhood, but memories of the *Shoah*, particularly the disappearance of my parents and of almost all the members of the very large family that was theirs in Poland, haunts me to this day.

REMEMBER ME

by Irene N. Watts

Marianne Kohn has escaped Hitler's Germany by Kindertransport. Now safely in England, she is still haunted by the memories of the past. Marianne's foster mother is unsympathetic to her fears. The girl's anxiety for her family and her efforts to bring her parents to England are met with hostility.

Chapter Five
"I'm fine"

Marianne woke up on her first Saturday in England and stared at the overhead lightbulb. It was on. She must have fallen asleep before she'd switched it off.

She was starving. When she went down to the kitchen, it was lovely and warm. A place had been set for Marianne at one end of the scrubbed table.

"Porridge," said Gladys, as she placed a bowl of some kind of gray pudding in front of Marianne. "Here, I'll show you." She sprinkled sugar over the top and poured milk from a glass bottle, then swiftly cut triangles of toast and arranged them in a silver toast rack on a tray and left the room.

Marianne eagerly spooned up the porridge. It was lucky that Gladys wasn't there just then because the first mouthful almost made Marianne gag. Quickly she scraped the food into the sink and turned on the tap, so that by the time Gladys came back, Marianne was sitting down again, the empty bowl in front of her. She could almost smell the warm crusty rolls her mother always served for breakfast, with homemade black cherry jam. She wanted to be with her so much that she had to dig her nails into her palms to stop from crying.

Marianne tried to imagine what her mother was doing. She might be in Düsseldorf by now. After they'd got the notice from Mrs. Schwartz saying she wouldn't allow Jewish tenants in the building anymore, Mutti had said she'd leave as soon as she'd packed up.

"I don't think I can bear it," Marianne said, and only Gladys' stare of surprise and her "what did you say?" made her realize she'd spoken aloud, and in German. *I mustn't do that again. Do the other kids from the transport feel this mixed up?*

Mrs. Abercrombie Jones walked into the kitchen, her coat over her arm.

"Good morning, Mary Anne."

"Good morning, Aunt . . ." Marianne had forgotten how to pronounce the "aunt's" name.

"Aunt Vera," prompted her sponsor. "Gladys, we are leaving now."

Leaving? Who is leaving? Leaving means going away. Am I being returned to Liverpool Street Station?

Marianne heard her name – she was supposed to do something. *What is it?* Marianne knew she had to pay more attention. She'd missed most of their conversation. She didn't know why her thoughts kept drifting.

Mrs. Abercrombie Jones left the kitchen.

Gladys put a duster in Marianne's hand. "You dust downstairs. Come on, I'll show you."

Marianne was afraid she might break something, or put things back in the wrong place, and only dusted around objects, not daring to move anything. At last she was done and could go upstairs, make her bed, and settle down to write home.

Marianne didn't want to upset her mother. She was determined to hide her homesickness and how much she wished she'd never come. Instead, she tried to write cheerfully.

> 12 Circus Road,
> St. John's Wood,
> London, NW8
> England

> 3 December, 1938

Dear Mutti,

I arrived safely. I liked the boat. I have my own room at the top of the house. There is a garden. I have plenty to eat and can understand a lot of English words. Mrs. Abercrombie Jones, the lady who took me in, says I can start school on Monday.

I was so happy when I found your letter. I'll remember what you wrote about looking at the same sky even though we are living in different countries.

The scene in the train compartment, when the Gestapo emptied the contents of the suitcases on the floor, flashed in front of Marianne. She'd never forget the greedy eyes of the man who'd stolen Werner's stamp album. Funny how she could remember the names of every one of the children she'd traveled with, yet found it so hard to recall Aunt Vera's.

Marianne tried not to think about the way the Gestapo officer had hit her bear across his knee, the way he'd wrenched off the head of Sophie's doll. She relived the moment when she'd edged her foot forward to cover the letter from her mother that had slipped out of its hiding place in the sleeve of Marianne's party dress.

Marianne got out of bed and ran across the cold floor to get her mother's letter from its hiding place in the lining in her suitcase. She smoothed the page carefully and read her mother's words:

My dearest daughter,

You will be far away from me when you read this letter. It is so hard to let you go. I watched you sleeping last night as though you were still a small baby. I wished I could change my mind and keep you here, but that would be too selfish.

You are going to a better, safer life. Here, there might be no life at all. One day you will understand why I had to let you go. If only we had more time together. Someone else will lengthen your clothes, buy you new shoes, tie your hair. Did it grow into curls as you always hoped it would? I miss you already. I will miss having to nag you for coming in late. I will miss complaining about your messy room, or you not doing your homework. I will miss your first grown-up party. Will you still love to dance?

Please try to understand, Marianne, why I must miss all your growing up, all these special things. Because, I love you. I want to give you the very best life there is, and that means a chance to grow up in a free country. Here there is only fear.

I pray that you, and all the children whose parents send them away, will find loving families. I will think of you every day, and wish for your happiness, and that you will grow up into a good honorable person.

Wherever you are, wherever I am, at night we will be looking at the same sky.

Always, your loving Mutti

She folded up the letter carefully and put it back in her suitcase. She knew she would never own anything more precious than this. Marianne had to wipe her eyes before she could continue writing her own letter.

"I'm fine." *Will Mutti know this is a lie? I'm not fine. I'm afraid.* Not afraid of being beaten up in the streets by gangs of Hitler Youth, nor the kind of fear she'd felt when she saw the body of the man tumbling down from the window of his house in the square. This was a kind of fear she'd never experienced before – wanting to cry all the time because she didn't know what to do, or what was expected of her; not knowing how long it would be before Mutti could come for her; afraid because she did not belong anywhere and was trying not to show how strange she felt in this English house.

"Please give my love to <u>everyone</u>." Marianne underlined the word twice. "Don't worry about me. I know you'll try to come here soon.

Much love and many kisses,

From Marianne"

When Marianne asked Gladys where to post her letter, Gladys said, "Turn right at the end of the street. The pillar-box is around the corner; it's red." Marianne found the way easily.

She'd be brave, walk on and explore a bit. There was nothing else for her to do. She hadn't seen any books or games when she was dusting.

Marianne walked along the High Street. The shops were crowded, and so were the pavements. Some windows already had Christmas decorations in them. Marianne looked for a bookshop, and found one. It was much bigger than the one her father used to work in. She looked eagerly at the display. At the top of a pyramid of books was a familiar red cover – *Mein Kampf* by Adolf Hitler. The black swastika looked huge. It stared at her.

Suddenly Marianne began to run, pushing through the shoppers as if Hitler himself were after her. She did not stop until she had a pain in her side, and her lungs hurt. She leaned against some park railings to catch her breath. She must stop being so silly. Her father always talked about "freedom to choose." This was a free country, so bookshops could sell anything they wanted to. But why choose that book?

Marianne went inside the park. It didn't look like a place to be afraid of. A river wound in curves through the green lawns. Fat ducks swam among reeds, or sheltered under overhanging trees. Unexpected fountains, small ornate bridges, and paving stones in intricate patterns surprised her. A small girl bowling a red hoop just avoided crashing into her. "Be careful," called the girl's mother. Marianne knew what the words meant from the woman's gesture. She thought longingly of the times she'd groaned when Mutti told her to be careful. She'd give anything to hear it now.

An old lady was feeding pigeons. She made room on the bench for Marianne to sit down, then carefully poured some birdseed from a paper bag into Marianne's hand. A pigeon alighted on Marianne's wrist. A small boy with a red kite ran around making bird noises and the pigeons scattered. The old lady said, "Goodbye, dear," and left.

It was getting cold; other people were leaving. This was the first time Marianne could remember sitting on a bench that wasn't marked FOR ARYANS ONLY – the first time she'd been in a park where Jews could sit anywhere they liked, not only on yellow benches. It was late; the afternoon was over.

When she found her way out of the gates, she didn't know which way to go. She must have come out through a different entrance. It was almost dark. *I'm lost.* An English policeman walked past her. *Is it safe to speak to him?*

"Please," Marianne sobbed.

He turned and walked back and looked at her. "Now then," he said, "no need to cry. Did someone hurt you?"

Marianne hadn't realized she was crying. She shook her head, wiped her eyes, and fumbled for the piece of paper with her address on it. The policeman took it. He spoke too fast for Marianne to understand more than a few "lefts" and "rights."

"Please, I don't understand," she said.

"Follow me," said the policeman, and walked her all the way home to her gate.

Aunt Vera's horrified face, when Gladys opened the front door and said, "Here she is, Madam," told Marianne that she must have seen the policeman. "Where have you been? What will the neighbors think?" She sounded very angry. Not worried – angry – embarrassed angry.

"Sorry," said Marianne. "I lose the way."

Aunt Vera talked loudly at her for a long time before sending her into the kitchen for tea. Marianne was in disgrace.

SURVIVOR STORY:
The Toy Steam Engine

by Serge (Wajnryb) Vanry

The boy has come by the toy store window almost every afternoon, stopping to stare at the bright Christmas lights and decorations that frame the display of mechanical building sets and miniature engines. It is a cold winter day, in a strange city, in an unfamiliar region, and he is shivering in his wooden-soled shoes and his borrowed ill-fitting coat as he studies the finely crafted parts of the shiny, polished, small-scale working model of a steam engine. His nose rests close to the frosted glass; his eyes caress every detail of this magnificent machine. His imagination fancies the burning of fuel pellets and the hiss of escaping steam as the pistons begin to push the flywheel and set all the parts in motion.

Suddenly he remembers who and where he is. He looks around quickly, making sure that no stranger notices him, then moves on into the icy wind and the darkness of his life. He remembers the admonitions to be careful, to be as invisible as possible, to not talk to strangers and to remember his false identity if questioned. The eleven-year-old boy is a fugitive. Loneliness weighs heavily on him for he is by himself, having run away when the gendarmes came to take away his family. He is now staying with kind and courageous people who took him in and provide him with the basic necessities. Nights are particularly long and troubled, and tears flow often when he thinks of his loved ones and the loss of their warmth and affection.

The boy returns to the toy store as often as possible because that steam engine represents all the things that were his before he became an instant "orphan." The engine is a dream, a fantasy of his past, a past that he can revisit when he looks at the toy store display. This bit of sunshine makes the despair and the feeling of abandonment that loom over him more bearable. He imagines the machine at full speed; he remembers all the elements of his life before the darkness and the terror.

More than fifty years have passed. A graying, balding man passes by a hobby store, far removed from the toy store of his youth. He is in a new country, where places and people do not remind him of his painful past. He stops, attracted by building sets, and suddenly sees steam engines, as gloriously enticing as the ones in his childhood dreams. Engines just as perfect, just as polished, just as elegant, demanding his attention, triggering a flood of feelings and memories. He enters the store, his heart beating rapidly, his hands clammy; he asks to see the toy engine from the window display. He barely hears the sales clerk's remarks, the fact that these trains are made in Germany and therefore finely crafted and designed. He hesitates. *Should I if it is German?* "Actually," he says to himself, "this is for me alone and I will not share it with anybody else, although I may allow my family to watch as I demonstrate it."

The toy engine sits on the kitchen table, looking totally unlike the childhood image the man had carried with him most of his life. This machine works when filled with water, heated with pellets; hot steam working pistons, flywheel, and steam whistle. . . . His children and grandchildren are excited and impressed, hovering over the toy, wanting to try their hand at it.

The gray-haired man is not disappointed by his lack of enthusiasm for his purchase, realizing that in this country, he has gained more than he lost. He will keep the steam engine to remember a time when the world went mad.

III

Selection

SURVIVOR STORY:
Auschwitz

by Leo Lowy

I was born in 1928 in Carpathia, in the city of Berehovo near Mukachevo, which is known for its rabbis. I came from a close family. I had five sisters, including one who was my twin. My oldest sister was married with a child. I had uncles and aunts who lived in the same city. We had a normal life, observed Jewish traditions and went to services on Friday night. I attended both a regular and a Jewish school.

The Holocaust

Things started changing in 1938. The Czech government ceased to exist, the Hungarians took power and I began learning Hungarian in school. There were those in the Hungarian régime who were obviously anti-Semitic. They started robbing Jewish families, taking their belongings. They even had their own swastika. They caused us a lot of problems.

By 1940–41, things that were happening seemed abnormal because they happened so suddenly. I remember that panic set in because we were given news about an uncle and aunt and their family who were taken from their home and sent to a place in Poland because they did not have proper documents. News filtered out that they were executed, but we couldn't believe it until it was proven by one of the escapees.

I was taken by the Hungarians from Berehovo to a brick factory in 1943. Then we were transported by cattle car, a hundred or more to a car, to Auschwitz. There was little food, no facilities; they slammed the door shut, and we rolled along for days. We arrived in Auschwitz in the middle of the night; they didn't open the doors until nine or ten in the morning. We had to listen to the soldiers hollering and the dogs barking. I will never forget the cries and the stench of that car.

Soon we were lined up along the tracks and soldiers went up and down, shouting and looking for people with abnormalities. First, they were looking for twins, but because of the commotion, or perhaps out of fear, my parents never volunteered that I was a twin. Luckily for us our neighbor, who was standing beside us, called out that she had twins and, pointing to us, said that my sister and I were twins.

We were taken to a hospital in Birkenau. We were told that everything would be all right and that we would be reunited with our parents, but something didn't seem right, and I was scared. I tried to find out what was happening. Someone showed us the chimneys and told me what was happening in this place. I didn't tell my sister and, from that day on, I never took my eyes off those chimneys.

We were taken to a separate place and visited by Dr. Mengele, who was called Dr. Death by the other inmates. For about nine months, Mengele and many other doctors examined my sister and I, sometimes alone and sometimes together. They injected us with fluids and took samples from us.

I saw beatings and corpses brought in from the camps. I recognized some of these people from my hometown.

Liberation

In January 1945, we were marched in the heavy snow and bitter cold from Birkenau to Auschwitz, which was about five miles away. I was able to escape, and hid in a basement. I didn't know that my twin sister was in the same group, and she, by a miracle, ran into three of our sisters in Auschwitz. My sisters went on the Death March from Auschwitz and were liberated by the Americans four months later. Unfortunately, except for my twin, my other sisters were so weak that they died within a week after being liberated.

If it wasn't for the fact that my sister and I were twins, we wouldn't be here today.

HOLDING HIM

by Deborah Schnitzer

they stood by the side of the transport holding hands

their father told them
"stay together
hold onto each other;
whatever happens
do not let go!"

when the girl knew she'd forgotten
she picked up her younger brother's hand.
they stood
her cloak frayed at the hood
his face turned down
like a bed at night
if someone was looking for them
it was death

in the mud that circled their ankles
and the wind that unwrapped them
nobody lifted a finger

the gravel spit by the transport stoned them
and the rain bruised them
when they fell down she lay like a glove

holding him

NONE IS TOO MANY

by Jason Sherman

> *Canada did not welcome Jewish refugees before or immediately after the Second World War. It was 1947 before the government admitted one thousand one hundred and twenty-three war orphans. A Blessing in Disguise is from the play None Is Too Many, based on the book by Irving Abella and Harold Troper.*

A Blessing in Disguise

KING: I am shaken, gentlemen.

HAYES: Ottawa, November 1938. Prime Minister William Lyon Mackenzie King meets with his Quebec Lieutenant Ernest Lapointe, Minister of Mines & Resources Thomas Crerar, and Frederick Blair, head of the Immigration Branch.

KING: Shaken. The Hebrew race is being perse-cuted, we have been asked by the world to open our doors, and what have we done? Nothing. That is what we have done. Now we wake up to this. *(looking at newspaper:)* "Jewish synagogues burned, looted by German mobs."

Kristallnacht, they call it. "In the earlier stages Jews were attacked and beaten. Some 15,000 were sent to prisons or concentration camps. In their panic and misery about 50 men and women attempted suicide; 20 succeeded." Dear dear dear. What a position the race is in. Gentlemen, the time has come for us to do what is right, and just, and Christian. It will be difficult politically, of course, but we must do something.

LAPOINTE: Difficult, Mr. Prime Minister? It will cost us the country.

CRERAR: Not so, not so.

KING: Let the man speak, Tom.

LAPOINTE: Of course I sympathize with the plight of these poor people. This country has joined others in sending a note of protest and concern to Berlin. Beyond that, we are bound by practicalities. The people of Quebec are against Jewish immigration. Editorials every day warn about the effects of an increased Jewish presence on our streets. I do not say that these feelings are right – or wrong – merely the reality. And a further reality is that Premier Duplessis will use the refugees as props in his little morality play. I guarantee you that for every refugee that sets foot on Quebec soil, there will be a hundred thousand lost votes for the Liberal party in –

CRERAR: This is –

LAPOINTE: In Quebec. And as the party goes in Quebec –

CRERAR: I cannot –

KING: Thomas, please.

LAPOINTE: So it will go in the rest of the country.

CRERAR: What sort of a nation do we wish to build here, gentlemen? Mr. Prime Minister, Immigration was shuffled from one ministry to the next until it finally landed with me in Mines and Resources. Mines and Resources. What sort of a message is that to send to the nations of the world, when we place people in among the rocks and minerals?

KING: They are resources, Tom, let's not get stuck on a word.

CRERAR: No, indeed. Let us not get stuck – on words. Gentlemen, the time has come for action, and action is what we shall take. Having consulted with the Jewish members of parliament, I –

LAPOINTE: What?

CRERAR: I have decided to announce that Canada, following the lead of Australia, will take in 10,000 Jewish –

LAPOINTE: Impossible!

CRERAR: 10,000 Jewish refugees *forthwith*.

LAPOINTE: We were not consulted.

KING: This is quite improper, Thomas.

LAPOINTE: I will resign if you make this announcement.

CRERAR: Here is a pen.

KING: Gentlemen! *Gentlemen*. Thomas, you have no authority to – *we* have no authority to make this announcement.

BLAIR: Quite so.

CRERAR: We are the bloody government!

KING: The bloody *federal* government, Minister Crerar. Immigration is a shared jurisdiction; we must consult with the provinces on this.

BLAIR: And not the Jewish members of parliament.

CRERAR: What's that, Mr. Blair?

BLAIR: I say –

CRERAR: I heard you. Bear in mind that I am the Minister responsible for immigration, *Mister* Blair. You are not here to make policy, sir, but to follow it.

BLAIR: Quite so. I am merely a humble civil servant. I do not make policy. But I do see its effects. Keeping the refugees out of Canada is doing them a favor, even if they can't see it. Their presence would in fact foment anti-Semitism.

CRERAR: Which will disappear once the Canadian people see that the refugees are human beings just like any other.

BLAIR: The Jews do not consider themselves to be human beings like any other. They consider themselves to be the Chosen People, which is why they prefer to keep themselves separate from the rest of us.

KING: That is a rather baroque argument, Mr. Blair.

BLAIR: Then allow me to make another. We are trying to build a country here, a country comprising one people. The Canadian people. These refugees refuse to fit in. They stick to *their* ways. And their ways are not very . . . Canadian. If they were to divest themselves of certain of their habits, I am sure they could be just as popular as our Scandinavians. They speak of persecution, as if it occurs in a vacuum. The fact is that their "persecution" stretches back some 2,000 years, during which time not once have they paused long enough to ask themselves why they are the subject of such persecution. Perhaps if they did, and honestly, they would come to the realization that they owe their oppression to none other than themselves. You think you are doing the Jewish people a favor by lobbying for their admission. I tell you the opposite is true.

LAPOINTE: Clearly, this issue needs further study.

CRERAR: No, Minister Lapointe. No further study is needed. I have heard enough. The Canadian people stand behind me.

KING: Indeed? Stand aside, Thomas, and show them to me.

(pause)

I believe I spoke too soon, from feeling rather than thought. On reflection, instead of allowing this horrible pogrom to become the catalyst for unwanted immigration, we should look upon it as a blessing in disguise.

CRERAR: A blessing?

KING: The nations of the free world have responded with such revulsion that Hitler will have no choice but to cease and desist from any further action against the Jews. In time, this terrible night will vanish from memory. The Jews will be permitted to return to their homes.

Hitler . . . I sat there with him. Asked him some very blunt questions. And he answered me. An interesting fellow. A good man, I think. You can tell, from the eyes, how good a person is.

Good day, gentlemen.

HANA'S SUITCASE:
A True Story

by Karen Levine

Who is Hana Brady, Jewish orphan, born 1931? What is her life story? Inspired to find out, Fumiko journeys across Europe and North America. Gradually she pieces together clues about the young owner of the suitcase with the polka-dot lining.

Tokyo, Japan, Winter 2000

Really, it's a very ordinary looking suitcase. A little tattered around the edges, but in good condition.

It's brown. It's big. You could fit quite a lot in it – clothes for a long trip, maybe. Books, games, treasures, toys. But there is nothing inside it now.

Every day children come to a little museum in Tokyo, Japan to see this suitcase. It sits in a glass cabinet. And through the glass you can see that there is writing on the suitcase. In white paint, across the front, there is a girl's name: Hana Brady. A date of birth: May 16, 1931. And one other word: *Waisenkind*. That's the German word for orphan.

The Japanese children know that the suitcase came from Auschwitz, a concentration camp where millions of people suffered and died during the Second World War between 1939 and 1945. But who was Hana Brady? Where did she come from? Where was she traveling to? What did she pack? How did she become an orphan? What kind of girl was she and what happened to her?

The children are full of questions. So is the director of the museum, a slender young woman with long black hair named Fumiko Ishioka.

Fumiko and the children gently take the suitcase out of the glass case and open it. They search the side pockets. Maybe Hana left something that would be a clue. Nothing. They look under the polka-dot lining. There are no hints there either.

Fumiko promises the children to do everything she can to find out about the girl who owned the suitcase, to solve the mystery. And for the next year, she becomes a detective, scouring the world for clues to the story of Hana Brady.

Theresienstadt, May 1942

The train trip was quiet, uneventful. People seemed to keep to themselves, lost in their own thoughts and fears about the future. After a few hours, the train came to an abrupt halt. The doors were flung open and the frightened passengers standing nearest to the doors could see the sign reading "Bohusovic Station." Hana squinted in the sunlight as she and George lugged their suitcases off the train. There, at the station, they were instructed to walk the rest of the way to the Theresienstadt fortress.

It was only a few kilometers, but their suitcases were cumbersome and heavy. Should we leave some things here, Hana and George wondered, to lighten our load? No, everything in their suitcases was precious, the only reminders of the life they used to have. George carried one suitcase. The other one they put on a moving cart, pushed by prisoners.

Hana and George approached the entrance to the walled fortress and joined a lineup. Everyone was wearing a yellow star, just like them.

At the front of the line, a soldier asked people for their name, age and place of birth. Boys and men were being sent in one direction, girls and women in another. "Where are they going?" Hana asked George. More than anything else, she was afraid of being separated from her brother. "Can I stay with you?" she pleaded.

"Be quiet, Hana!" George told his sister. "Don't make a fuss."

When they reached the front of the line, the soldier stared at them. "Where are your parents?" he demanded.

"They are, uh, in another, uh, camp," George stammered. "We hope that here we might be reunited."

The soldier wasn't interested in conversation. He wrote down their names on index cards and searched their suitcases for money and jewelry. Then he slammed the bags shut. "To the left!" he ordered George. "To the right!" he ordered Hana.

"Please can I stay with my brother?" Hana asked.

"Move! Now!" the soldier ordered. What Hana feared most was about to happen. George gave her a quick hug. "Don't worry," he said. "I'll find you as soon as I can." Holding back tears, Hana picked up her suitcase and followed the other girls to *Kinderheim* (children's home) L410, a large barrack for girls that was to be Hana's home for the next two years.

IV

Ghetto

SURVIVOR STATEMENT

RUTH KRON SIGAL

I was five in 1941 when the Germans came to Shavli, Lithuania, where I had been born. Together, with my parents and my two-year-old sister, Tamara, we were forced into the ghetto. On November 3, 1943, during a *Kinderaction* (roundup of Jewish children), Tamara and I were hidden in the house of a relative. We were apprehended. I was released, but Tamara was deported to Auschwitz. I am still haunted by the vision of my baby sister on that truck, with her arms outstretched towards me. I was taken in by a Catholic couple who changed my name, taught me to speak fluent Lithuanian (at home we had spoken mostly Yiddish and Russian) and brought me up as a Catholic. We were liberated by the Russians in 1944.

THE OLD BROWN SUITCASE:

A Teenager's Story of
War and Peace

by Lillian Boraks-Nemetz

*Slava's happy home life has been
destroyed by war. Soon after
Liberation, the Lenski family
emigrate to Canada. Here, while
trying to make a new life, Slava
is troubled by the dark memories
of her Holocaust past.*

Chapter Seven
Escape

I am nine.

In the months to come I resume playing with the kids in
the courtyard, but soon even that comes to an end.

The latest orders from the Germans are that everyone
who wants to survive must work. Father already works for
the Werkschutz, in the workshop of the Security Force. He
arranges for Mother to work at one of the Wehrmacht
workshops set up in the Ghetto by the German army,
to manufacture uniforms and other things that the soldiers need.

Mother and I walk each morning to the Schultz Company.
The room where Mother works is very long, filled with tables,
sewing machines and workers.

Children are not supposed to be here, but Father makes special arrangements for me to get in, as long as I make myself as inconspicuous as possible.

All day Mother sews fur collars to be put on German uniforms. I hide on the floor under the table and try to help by picking up pieces of fur and thread, but it is hot and uncomfortable under the table. For lunch, the workers are given soup and sometimes a piece of bread. The soup looks like brown water and is tasteless, and the bread is stale. But it is all we have to eat for the entire ten-hour day. I am always hungry these days, so I feel lucky to have even that. The hunger makes us weak and often I see Mother swaying on her feet from exhaustion.

When we walk to and from work, we see terrible things in the Ghetto. Children beg in the street. Dirt and garbage pile up and rats scuttle in dark corners. We see a man shot because he refuses to bow to a German officer. We see another man hung naked on a tree by soldiers, who laugh at his nakedness. Old people are shot to death simply because the German soldiers consider them useless.

The Ghetto is overcrowded. More than four hundred thousand people are living in a space where only a hundred and sixty thousand used to live. But now the German soldiers want to send us away – those who have not died from sickness or starvation. The soldiers begin to raid different parts of the Ghetto and take people away. No one knows when their street or home will be raided next. Just in case, we keep our suitcases packed and ready. My own brown suitcase is beginning to look a little battered.

One early morning, they come to our building. We can hear their boots march into the courtyard. They shout in German, banging on doors. We wait in our room, until they come, their black polished boots echoing up the long corridor. They get closer and closer and then stop. A heavy fist pounds our door. It bursts open and a red-faced soldier rushes into our room. He levels his rifle at us.

"*Juden raus!*" (Get out, Jews!) he hollers, and his rifle follows us as we take our suitcases.

We file out of the building and join the others in the courtyard. Everyone lines up with their belongings at a table set up in the center of the courtyard. As the officers check everyone's identity cards, they tell them to line up in two rows. When our turn comes the officer who checks our cards ignores the fact that my parents work for the German Shop and orders us to line up at the left. My parents say nothing. The soldiers herd us out onto the street, where there is already a long column of people waiting. Jews, young, old and middle-aged. All look shabby, sick and starved. We line up with them and wait.

People whisper, some are sitting on their bundles.

"Where are we going?" they ask one another, "What will happen to us?"

A man in a torn coat asks Father, "Do you know about the labor camps? They say that it's better there. If you work you survive."

"There are so many rumors," answers Father. "People are taken to a collection place called Umschlagplatz, and then deported by train to some resettlement camp in the east. I am sure that is where we are going. But I don't know exactly what happens when we get there."

The soldiers order us to start walking. They walk alongside, pointing their rifles at the moving throng. Though it is
early fall, the day is cold and rainy. My coat and shoes are soon
soaked through.

"Faster," shouts the soldier who ordered us from our
room. His red face scowls out from under his steel helmet. He
shoves an old couple forward with the butt of his rifle, and
they fall to the ground. They lie there, while the soldier orders
us to walk over them.

Another soldier beats a woman with a black truncheon.
She falls screaming to the ground. The soldier forces her to
get up and continue without her belongings.

I stumble, the soldier screams at me and hits me on the
shoulder. I fall. Father instantly picks me up and steadies me.
"Be brave," he whispers.

I don't feel brave. My knees are bloody, and my shoulder
hurts but I still hang on to the brown suitcase. I feel like an
animal who is being punished for something. But what did I
do? They drive us along in a pony-like trot. We cower beneath
the menacing batons and guns, shoulders hunched over.

There are people lying on the sidewalks. Some dead, some
still half alive. Blood stains the pavement. Starved children
with swollen bellies and bony legs hover next to the buildings,
watching us pass.

Suddenly the column comes to a halt as shots boom out. I
am lost in a maze of filthy coats and rags. Blue Stars of David
flicker before my eyes. People push against me. It's hard to
keep my balance. Then I find myself next to Mother, who is
carrying my crying sister. I clutch Mother's arm with my free
hand. When I finally let go, there are red marks in her flesh,

where I have dug my nails. Father appears at my side and pulls Mother and me out of the lineup. "Run, run, quickly, through that gate!" He thrusts us forward. We run through an arched gateway into a quiet courtyard. No one follows us. Father leads us through an open door into a deserted apartment. We huddle in its dark corridor for what seems a long time.

Finally, Father breaks the silence, wiping the perspiration off his forehead. "It was a chance we had to take. We were only five minutes away from the Umschlagplatz and the trains. I have seen them pack those cattle cars. They put so many people in each, how can they breathe? And who knows where they go from there. I've heard that they separate parents from children, and that no one comes back." Father's voice is weary. Basia is asleep, and Mother sits on the floor against a wall, with her eyes closed. We haven't eaten all day.

When all appears quiet, we leave and learn that we must find a new apartment because our part of the Ghetto has been liquidated.

Several weeks later Father hears a rumor that all the children in the Ghetto will be taken from their parents and sent away. No one knows where.

Father and Mother decide that my sister and I must leave the Ghetto. There are many questions I want to ask, but the troubled look on my parents' faces keeps me silent.

Each night I lie awake, terrible thoughts flooding my mind. Each day I wait for Father to tell me that I must leave. There is hardly any food, even at the factory. Except for the walk to Schultz, I never go outside any more and it's almost spring.

I awake one morning with a fever.

My head hurts, my body is on fire, through a mist I hear voices saying, "It's measles. She can't go anywhere." I toss and turn and sweat for days. Once when I wake up I see Mother standing over the cot. She is holding Basia, who is dressed in a coat and hat.

"Say good-bye to your sister. She is going away," says Mother quietly. Through a daze I try to focus on the bundle in a brown wool coat and a white hat with bunny ears. Two big blue eyes in a little face look down at me. What does she want from me? Can't she see I am sick? I push her away, and turn towards the wall.

In the morning I wake up feeling better. The fever seems to have gone. The sun is shining outside. Where is everyone? I look around the room and see that Basia's bed is gone. I run to the wardrobe, and see an empty shelf where her things once were. My God, I didn't know she was leaving for good. I didn't even say good-bye.

That evening my parents make sure that my brown suitcase is properly packed. Although it is so full that it is hard to close, I refuse to part with my books and my sunflower costume. I beg and they let me keep them.

"Now don't be frightened," says Father almost cheerfully. "You will have to leave soon, but I don't know when."

I go to sleep feeling comforted, but wake with a start. Someone is shaking me.

"Hurry, hurry," says Father. Mother dresses me quickly and hugs me. As she says good-bye her voice is thick with held-back tears.

A minute later, Father and I are shivering on a misty street. It is dawn.

The street is deserted.

We walk quickly. I ask no questions, for I know what we are doing. When we hear the rumble of a truck approaching, Father pulls me into a doorway. An army truck passes, and we continue walking.

We stop at a half-burnt building. Father pushes at the front door, which squeaks open, and we walk into a dark apartment. It is empty, and Father tells me to sit on my suitcase and wait.

"Don't be scared," he says. "I am waiting for someone." He paces up and down as if rehearsing some speech in his mind.

The door squeaks again, and I jump. A man walks in wearing the cap and badge of the Jewish Police Force of the Ghetto. Father greets him with a handshake, then takes a small jewelry box, a pair of leather gloves and some soap out of his pockets and hands them over. The man opens the jewelry box and in the dawn light something sparkles. It's Mother's diamond ring. The man stuffs the things in his coat and leaves. Father tells me to be patient. He tells me what I already know, that I am leaving the Ghetto.

I sit on my suitcase and keep silent. A rat scurries across the floor. Then another. I move my suitcase away from the squeaking rats, and Father stops pacing. He shoos away the rats and sits down next to me on the floor.

"You are going to your grandmother in the country, if all goes well," he says slowly.

Babushka! I will see Babushka! For a moment I am overcome with excitement. I feel brighter in a gloomy room. "Are you coming too, Papa?" I ask.

"No, darling girl, I am not. We would be too conspicuous, and I can't leave your mother alone. Just remember what I told you. We can't let the Germans win. We must survive. So when the time comes, you must follow my instructions perfectly."

"I will Papa," I mumble into his shoulder. My throat is all choked up with tears, but my eyes feel dry, and my body feels numb. I try not to cry.

As daylight approaches, I hear sounds I haven't heard for months. I hear streetcars and other vehicles, sounds of a normal city.

"Where are we, Papa?" I ask.

"Near the Ghetto gate to the other side," he replies, confirming my guess.

The policeman returns.

"It's all fixed," he says, "I gave them the goodies. They promised to pretend not to see her. But you know them, they can turn on you anytime. It's a chance you have to take. Good luck!" He salutes and leaves.

Father sits down on the floor and places his head in his hands. After a long moment, he gets up.

"We're leaving now. Remember what I told you," he says, taking my hand and my suitcase.

We leave the building and walk for several blocks. We stop and Father squeezes my hand tightly.

About half a block from us is a busy checkpoint in the Wall. Three soldiers in steel helmets hold rifles as if ready to shoot. They march back and forth in front of the large opening. Several Polish policemen in navy blue uniforms stand by the opening.

"This is the way out of the Ghetto, Slava. You are going to cross the line in a few minutes," Father says gravely. "In the pocket of your coat is a false identity card. The name on it is Irena Kominska. It says that you are a Catholic orphan from Warsaw. There will be a woman waiting for you on the other side. She will know you, and she will take you to Babushka's."

I am frozen. I say nothing. Father gives me the suitcase. My hand can barely hold it.

"When I tell you, start walking," he says, "walk through the checkpoint at a normal pace. Do not hesitate, or run. Above all do not turn around to look at me." He hugs me with tears in his eyes.

"Now go!"

I look at him for one last moment, let go of his hand, and begin the longest walk of my life.

I try to feel brave as I march towards the checkpoint. As I draw closer, the green German uniforms grow bigger, and the shiny buttons of the Polish police coats gleam in the sunlight. I arrive at the checkpoint and begin to walk through. The gendarmes and the police do not appear to notice me. As I walk straight ahead, they turn away. My knees feel weak, and heartbeat fills my throat, but I keep on walking. A few more steps and I am on the other side.

I hear shouting beside me.

"I know who you are, you little Jewess! I saw you!" A little boy in rags points his finger at me. I clutch my suitcase tightly as if it were Father's hand, expecting the worst. All of a sudden the shouting ceases as a tall woman in a gray suit grabs my hand, and pulls me into a side street.

She stops for a moment to take my suitcase from me. "You can call me Agnes," she says. "Don't be afraid." Only then do I remember that Father had said someone would be waiting for me on the other side.

We walk quickly now. The beggar boy is left behind, but I feel that the whole world is staring at us. We rush into a train station. Agnes shows the conductor our tickets and we climb into one of the cars. It is almost empty. A few minutes later the train pulls out of the station.

Agnes sits next to me. She is wearing a gray hat to match her suit. Her eyes are gray too, but large and bright. She is fair-haired. I wonder if she is Jewish. But then, I am fair-haired too.

It is my first train ride in two years. I sit on the wooden bench taking in things I haven't seen for so long. We pass open fields and forests, peasants on carts filled with straw, cows grazing in the pastures, and country houses with white curtains in the windows. The Ghetto wall is behind me. But I wish my parents and my sister were here. God knows when I will see them again.

I rest my head against the shoulder of the woman in a gray suit, as sleepiness overcomes me. It seems only an instant later that I hear someone say, "Wake up, Slava, we are almost there."

The voice is unfamiliar. Whose is it? Where am I?

I open my eyes and see Agnes. Oh, yes, I remember now. We are on the train going to Babushka. Agnes takes something out of her bag and hands it to me. A piece of bread and sausage. I almost swallow the food without chewing it. It's so good.

The sun shines brightly as the train moves through the peaceful countryside.

"You've slept for an hour and a half. We should be arriving soon," says Agnes. She tidies my hair and straightens my dress. "You want to look pretty for your grandmother," she says.

The train slows down and passes a white sign that says ZALESIE, then stops. Agnes takes my suitcase and we get off. The station is deserted. We walk to a wooden hut set back from the tracks, almost hidden by trees. Agnes slowly opens a door that squeaks.

It's a general store. An old woman sits half asleep in a rocking chair, a floral shawl around her shoulders and a kerchief on her head. She sees us and gets up with difficulty.

"What do you want?" she asks in rural Polish, eyeing us suspiciously. Her mouth is toothless and her voice harsh.

"Could you please direct us to Spokojna Street?" says Agnes.

"Who are you seeing there?" asks the woman.

"A friend," replies Agnes.

The old woman stares us up and down, then gives us instructions, pointing her bony finger out the window.

We come to a road, with small wooden houses on either side. As we pass by, curtains are pulled aside and faces look out at us. But there is no one to be seen on the road. No little kids play outside the houses. Only the occasional dog barks as we pass.

I am not afraid. I compare this peaceful village with the Ghetto, and happily breathe in the fresh country air. Then I think of my parents and my happiness ebbs.

We turn into Spokojna Street and stop at a white house, with a white wood fence around it.

A curtain is swept to one side, and a face looks out for a moment. Then the door of the house opens and Babushka runs. "Slava," she smiles, pecking me on the cheek, "my dear little Slava." Then she raises a finger to her lips, and draws us inside. There, in the privacy of drawn curtains, Babushka hugs me tearfully and sighs.

"The neighbors mustn't suspect anything," she says. "I told them that I promised to take in a friend's daughter."

Agnes stays for tea, and gives Babushka my papers.

A man comes in the house. He is bald, heftily built, with a red face and wears black, round-rimmed glasses. He is Babushka's husband, whom I have never met. His name is Vlad. He smiles in greeting and takes his tea.

Agnes says that she must leave.

"You are a very brave lady," says Babushka. "How will we ever thank you for bringing Slava to us?" She gives Agnes a jar of preserved pears for the road. The tall woman thanks her and kisses me good-bye.

"I hope to see you after the war is over," she says to me. "You are a brave little girl."

After Agnes is gone, Babushka takes my hand and leads me to my room. She beckons me to sit beside her on the bed. "Now, Slavenka, I want you to understand that we are in a very dangerous situation. I am Jewish and so are you, but no one must know, or they will report us to the Germans. Vlad is a Catholic and because we are married, they won't suspect him or me."

She strokes my blonde braids. "You look anything but Jewish, but you must still be careful whom you talk to. Say nothing about who you are or where you come from. As far as anyone here is concerned, you are just a visitor. People around here are so afraid of Germans that if they suspect one little thing, they'll report it. And then we are as good as dead. All three of us."

The room has a mirror on the wall. I look at myself and see a skinny runt with long blonde braids and a tattered navy blue dress. Surely that face isn't mine. It is a gray face, with sunken cheeks and black circles under its round green eyes. Babushka's hand gently strokes my hair. I close my eyes and turn weeping into her arms.

Babushka, who comes from Russia, often calls me Slavenka, the Russian diminutive of my name. I love her Russian accent when she speaks Polish, particularly the way she pronounces my name. The sound is like no other. It is soft and melodious. The love she feels for me sounds in the way she says it. Babushka is short, with very round hips, and large breasts. Her hair is a rusty gold because, I discover, she uses henna once a month. Already in her sixties, she does much physical work around the house and garden, and even carries home large tree branches from the forest for firewood. She has closets full of silk dresses, but never wears them because they are too good for Zalesie. Besides, she says, she is saving them for when the war is over. Then she plans to return to Warsaw, to her lovely apartment. Babushka has a big silver samovar, from which we drink our tea.

In the months that follow, I help Babushka with her chores, and she teaches me Russian. We begin with the poems by Alexander Pushkin, the great poet of Russia's golden age of literature. She also reads to me the Polish version of a Russian novel for young adults, *Princess Dzavacha*. I am fascinated with the heroine, whose name is Nina. She also had to part with her father and leave her home. She is a very brave girl.

Babushka also teaches me Russian folk songs. I learn to sing "Karobushka" and "Kalinka." We sing and dance together, while Vlad looks on and smokes his pipe. Then, when it is time for bed, she helps me wash up and tucks me in, singing a lullaby.

Even though I go to sleep calm and happy, there are many nights when I dream terrible nightmares. I wake up screaming. Babushka comes and takes me to her bed, where I fall asleep while she hums.

There are days, especially rainy autumn days, when I sit at home and just stare down the country road, aching for my parents. The look on Babushka's face tells me she understands.

Sometimes we go shopping. Food is scarce, so we line up for hours to get our ration of bread, one loaf per three days. We usually line up in front of the bakery, and the baker hands out the bread through the window. While in line, Babushka chats with her neighbors, about the weather and putting up preserves. They pay little attention to me, although from time to time some of them eye me with suspicion.

Our meals are simple and meager. We eat what Babushka and Vlad grow in their garden: vegetables and fruit in the summer, and in the winter, potatoes topped with cracklings. But we must ration ourselves carefully, or there will not be

enough for the three of us. I sit down to each meal only to feel
still hungry afterwards. Most of the food is given to Vlad
because Babushka says he is the master of the house.

Winter comes bringing ice and snow. Somewhere I had
lost my mittens, and my hands become red and chapped from
frost. I sit by the frozen window, behind a curtain of snow,
fingering the jagged flower patterns of ice. There has been no
word from my parents.

Spring arrives and still we hear nothing from my parents.
We wonder whether they are still in the Ghetto.

Then comes the terrible month of May, when night after
night the sky glows red in the direction of Warsaw. Vlad tells
us that the Ghetto is on fire. A handful of Jews refused to be
taken away in cattle cars like animals, and are resisting with
few guns and homemade weapons. In retaliation the Germans
are burning the Ghetto block by block.

One night, the sky is so red that the people of our village
gather outside their homes to watch.

A neighbor comments, "Look there, the Yids are frying,"
and laughs. I look at Babushka and see the horror in her eyes.
Here in this peaceful village, on this night, I feel as frightened
as I had felt in the Ghetto.

Later, I lie in bed and think about the way the neighbor
laughed at the suffering Jews. I picture the Jewish fighters
shooting down the enemy: they fall one by one, and the ignorant neighbor is among them. I can go to sleep now, feeling
proud that a handful of Jews had the courage to spit at the devil.

CHILDREN OF NIGHT

by Emanuel Gabriel

This play is based on the life story of Dr. Janusz Korczak. Korczak is the director of a Jewish orphanage in the Warsaw Ghetto. His devotion and sense of play help the children overcome the horrors that surround them. But how long can he protect them from danger?

KORCZAK: Children! (pause) Let's play a game.

GITTEL: Let's play outside then!

KORCZAK: Gittel, you know we can't play outside.

GITTEL: Why can't we?

KORCZAK: Because it's not safe. There are soldiers out there.

GITTEL: I hate them!

KORCZAK: No, Gittel, you don't hate them. You mustn't say that.

GITTEL: But I do! I do hate them! They're so mean and ugly. I hate the way they talk and march around and kick stuff over and scare people. I wouldn't call them soldiers. Soldiers fight other soldiers. What are they doing here? Why don't they leave us alone? Why do they have to act so big?

KORCZAK: I can't answer that, but you should still know that your own hatred will never make anyone else's go away.

GITTEL: Well I don't care! You don't make sense to me! Just let us play outside already!

KORCZAK: You heard me before. I said no. It is not safe to play outside now.

GITTEL: Then when can we?

KORCZAK: When I say so and that's enough said!

KESSLER: Perhaps we could return to . . .

KORCZAK: Excuse me, Maruk! Now listen, children. I am not asking you anymore, I am telling you. You have to learn. It's for your own good. In some cases you just have to trust me. I wouldn't make you do anything you'd be sorry for. You know that nobody likes taking a needle from the doctor but any fool would rather have that than a disease. Ignorance is a disease. The most deadly disease of them all. Ignorance is poison. It is contagious. It will spread through your mind, through your body, through your home, through your city, your country, the whole world if you give it a chance. And hatred is just like that, Gittel.

I know you don't like it, but these are important lessons to learn.

(There is a knock at the door)

When I was your age do you think that I wanted to learn? Absolutely not! Why I even . . .

BOINTSHE: Poppa! The door!

KORCZAK: (clapping his hands; children rise) Attention!

(KESSLER frantically moves to hide the map and exits through other door)

KORCZAK: (opening the door) Who is there,
                        please?

(MRS. FLEISHMAN enters holding the hand of a ten-year-
old boy, MOTL. He is dressed in a long overcoat and shorts,
long stockings that reach almost to the knee. On his head he
wears an oversized button-down cap. KORCZAK motions to
the CHILDREN to sit down)

MRS. FLEISHMAN: I am Mrs. Fleishman, Dr. Korczak.
                        The Jewish police sent me here. I
                        found this child . . . hidden . . . in the
                        Steinberg's shoe repair shop. He was
                        asleep, hunched up in a cupboard. I
                        heard banging earlier, but I did not
                        know what to do.

KORCZAK: So you brought him here.

(The child, MOTL, eases his way back towards the door)

MRS. FLEISHMAN: The Steinbergs reported for depor-
                        tation three days ago. No one even
                        knew that they had a child. I did not
                        know what to do . . . I don't even
                        know the boy. The Jewish police
                        said for me to . . . can you . . . can you
                        take him?

(KORCZAK looks uneasily at the children)

... Is it all right to leave him, then?

KORCZAK: Is it all right? Is that what you said? We are starving. We are overcrowded. They are sleeping two to a bed, some three to a bed. There is nothing to eat, but it's all right. I suppose one more soul won't make much of a difference. Little souls need other little souls to nourish them. And that is the one thing we have in abundance, as you can see.

MRS. FLEISHMAN: I'm sorry, I did not mean to be ... You see ... we are hiding my husband's mother. I would take him in, you know that, but the risk ... and the food ... and children. I did not know what to do.

KORCZAK: Tell me, have you found out his name?

MRS. FLEISHMAN: Yes, he says his name is Motl. That is about all he has told me.

KORCZAK: Motl, come here child. Don't be afraid. Look, these are all my children, aren't you, kids?

CHILDREN: (giggling) Yes, Poppa.

KORCZAK: You won't feel alone here. How old
                       are you? (silence) Well use your
                       fingers if your throat is sore. (no
                       reaction) Hmmm . . . (puts his arm
                       around Motl) Children, I want you to
                       meet your new brother, Motl. Be
                       kind to him and teach him whatever
                       rules we keep around here. Motl –
                       you do as your brothers and sisters
                       tell you; follow their example and you
                       will turn into a fine mensch, I
                       promise you. We learn and sing and
                       play lots of games here. Does that
                       sound like fun to you?

(MOTL is silent)

MRS. FLEISHMAN: It does, doesn't it, Motl?

KORCZAK: Sure it does. Now go over there and
                       join the family. (MOTL starts to
                       go) Wait. (KORCZAK reaches in his
                       pocket) Here is candy for you. All
                       children get one on their first day, but
                       don't go looking for any more tomor-
                       row, understand?

(MOTL walks over and sits down; the CHILDREN rush over to sit beside him; chatter)

MRS. FLEISHMAN: Thank you, Dr. Korczak.

KORCZAK: No thanks, please. You may go home now, he is in safe hands and in good company. (pause) Oh, by the way, I should inform you, in case you are unaware, that we may not allow visitors to the orphanage. If you were spotted coming or leaving here by the SS, they would assume that you were the mother of one of the children, and that would put your life or a child's in danger. I am sorry, but . . .

MRS. FLEISHMAN: I understand. I won't be back.

KORCZAK: However, we are performing in the Passover Cultural Festival a week this Thursday night, so if you would like to attend, by all means . . .

MRS. FLEISHMAN: Oh, we never leave the house at night anymore . . . but I will see if this once . . .

KORCZAK: I might even be able to arrange for
                    your little pot of gold here to appear
                    in our dramatic production.

MRS. FLEISHMAN: That would be wonderful. Thank you
                    so much. (starts to leave)

KORCZAK: I think it would be better, actually, if
                    you left through the back door – and
                    here, take this (gives her papers). If
                    anyone should stop you, tell them
                    that I summoned you from the street
                    to deliver these health certificates to
                    the hospital . . . say that my nurse is
                    sick today.

MRS. FLEISHMAN: Your nurse is sick. Yes, thank you.
                    (exits)

KORCZAK: Children! Children! We must turn to
                    the play immediately. For Motl's
                    benefit, will someone please explain
                    to him what our play is about?

CHILD: It's a play about Passover, about Moses
                    leading the children of Israel out
                    of slavery.

CHILD: From Egypt to the Promised Land!

KORCZAK: Right. Motl, do you know the story of Passover?

MOTL: My zayda told me. He was a rabbi. Let my people go! Let my people go! Let my people go!

KORCZAK: Well said, my boy. Would you like to be in our play?

MOTL: (shyly) I don't know. I've never been in a real play before.

CHILDREN: Come on, Motl.

MOTL: Do we get to dress up in costumes?

KORCZAK: Only the finest . . . brought by camels directly from the Sultan's palace.

MOTL: Do I get to wear a beard?

KORCZAK: If you cannot grow one, absolutely.

MOTL: Well . . .

KORCZAK: Well . . .

MOTL: Yes!

CHILDREN: Hooray!

KORCZAK: Good boy. Let me see what part I can
                   give you. Oh, don't tell me . . . there's
                   only one left. How would it be, if . . .

(ADAM CZERNIKOV abruptly enters, preceding a Nazi
officer)

                   Attention!

(The CHILDREN rise, face the NAZI, take off their caps,
bow and say, "Good day, sir." MOTL at first remains seated
and perplexed, but then, upon observing the others, he leaps
out of his seat and rushes over to the NAZI. He removes
his cap, bows, and enthusiastically repeats the greeting and
the gesture)

MOTL: Good day, sir! Good day, sir! Good
                   day, sir! Good day, sir! Good day, sir!
                   Good day, sir!

NAZI: Enough!

(MOTL begins to laugh, at first nervously but then graduat-
ing to a peak of hysteria)

                   Stop it!

KORCZAK: (shouting) Motl! Enough! (shakes him, then turns to the NAZI) Please excuse the boy . . . we just got him today . . . back from the hospital, that is. He is not completely recovered . . . still in a state of shock. Sit down here, boy, and be still. (seats him on a bench)

NAZI: He was ill you say, and they have released him back in your custody? He could have typhus.

KORCZAK: No, sir, it was only a fever. Nothing more.

NAZI: Nonsense! It could be infectious.

KORCZAK: No, sir, that is not possible. You see I have thoroughly examined the child, and as a doctor I can assure you that . . .

NAZI: Please, Dr. Korczak, you cannot assure me of the time of day. This . . . creature is . . . unsanitary, and as a carrier of germs could infect the entire population of your building.

KORCZAK: You should know, Herr Kommandant, that our building is not only a building,

but a Home, and in our Home the sick
are nursed back to health and disease
is not given the slightest opportunity
to spread. Not the slightest.

NAZI: Even so, this one will return with me.

KORCZAK: But you can't just take . . . the boy . . .

NAZI: I can't what, Dr. Korczak?

CZERNIKOV: Excuse me, Herr Kommandant, but
                 it is true . . . it was only a fever.
                 The report came into my office just
                 this morning.

NAZI: Are you quite sure of that, Mr.
                 Czernikov?

CZERNIKOV: Yes. I don't have the report with me
                 but it should still be on my desk.

NAZI: You will show me that report later,
                 Mr. Czernikov.

CZERNIKOV: Yes, sir, of course. Dr. Korczak, the
                 Kommandant has graciously con-
                 sented to approve the Cultural Night.

KORCZAK: That was kind of him.

CZERNIKOV: Providing that the affair is limited to no more than fifty attendants . . .

KORCZAK: Fifty?!

NAZI: (flatly) Fifty.

CZERNIKOV: . . . and is completely vacated by nine p.m. There are to be no speeches except for brief introductions. The Judenrat shall guarantee and impose order. If any rules are broken, the matter will be promptly reported and the disturber punished by death. Is this clear?

KORCZAK: Very clear, Mr. Czernikov.

NAZI: And you, Korczak, shall be held personally responsible for any incident that might occur. Mind that your little flock of goats doesn't wander off into trouble.

CZERNIKOV: Here is your permission slip. (opens door for NAZI) Good afternoon.

(Exit CZERNIKOV and NAZI)

KORCZAK: Good afternoon.

                     At ease, soldiers. Why don't you all
                     march out of here and play in the
                     other room for a while. You heard
                     what I said . . . go to the other room!

(CHILDREN are reluctant to move)

                     Go on! Move! (in anger) . . . Have
                     fun! . . . Play!

(CHILDREN exit somberly, except for MOTL, who hides
himself in a closet as KORCZAK turns to close the door)

                     They're entitled, aren't they? Or
                     need I request a permission slip
                     for them to play as well? (goes over
                     to his desk and begins to record
                     an entry in this diary) (writing)
                     "March 2. . . . New boy – Motl.
                     Parents unknown. Referred by a Mrs.
                     Fleishman. Indications of severe
                     withdrawal, malnutrition and incipient
                     hysteria. Incident with Kommandant –
                     interference with cultural activities.
                     Fifty spectators only. Nine p.m. curfew.

No more potatoes.

Very distressed . . . children learning to hate.

Gittel: 'You don't make sense to me.'

(He pauses, stops writing)

Good day, sir. (laughs) Good day, sir. Good day, sir. When the child laughs the tyrant trembles.

(He replaces diary in desk drawer. He reaches for writer's journal on top of shelf and resumes writing)

KORCZAK: "The child had discovered the ultimate weapon – laughter. It hung like a demonic presence in the room. The child laughed and blew the boots off the Kommandant's feet. He laughed again and blew the proud stiff uniform off the oppressor's back. He laughed again and again and left the tyrant naked . . . a pitiful figure made of glass that shattered into a thousand pieces.

And then it was over. The doctor stopped to pick up a piece of the broken glass. It was shaped like a heart. He held it to the sky and through the prism . . . revealed . . . was a rainbow. And chained to the rainbow was the figure of a man. A man . . . or a messenger? 'Moses? Moses, is that you?' the doctor cried. 'Why are you dressed in chains? Who in Heaven is holding you back? Come back, Moses . . . Moses, come back. . . . On your own if you must . . . Moses . . .'"

(A banging sound is heard from the closet)

MOTL: I want to play Moses!

(KORCZAK stops writing and runs over to the closet. He opens the door)

KORCZAK: Motl! What are you doing here? How long have you been in there?

MOTL: (bursts into tears) I . . . just . . . wanted . . . to be Moses.

KORCZAK: (embracing the boy) There, there, Motl, my little Moses. You don't have to cry.

MOTL: I'm scared!

KORCZAK: No! Moses scared? Motl, you must be brave if you want to be like Moses. Didn't your grandfather tell you how Moses stood up to the cruel Pharaoh and was not afraid to look him straight in the eye and say . . . well, you know what he said.

MOTL: Let my people go.

KORCZAK: That's right.

MOTL: My zayda knew Moses!

KORCZAK: Really?

MOTL: He was a rabbi.

KORCZAK: Yes, I know. What was his name?

MOTL: Zayda.

KORCZAK: I mean, what was his full name? Where did he come from? Where did you come from?

MOTL: (upset) I can't tell! I can't tell anybody! I made zayda a promise. My name is Motl, that's all.

V

In Flames

SURVIVOR STATEMENT

MALKA PISCHANITSKAYA

I come from the small village of Romanow in the Ukraine. When the Nazis arrived, Mother and I were forced to flee for our lives. We ran and hid from them in a barn. Our clothes were filthy and wet, but the hay kept us warm from the freezing cold outside.

When daylight came, in spite of my terror, hunger forced me outside to beg for bread, to keep Mother and me from starvation.

ROMEO AND JULIET IN SUCZORNO

by Martha Blum

"Shtetl" is the Yiddish word for the small East-European towns where Jews had lived for centuries. This is a fictional reconstruction of that world. It was totally annihilated by Nazi forces in World War II. Jews who lived according to the moral laws of the Bible were murdered, their homes looted, and their towns sent up in flames.

(The time is on the eve of the destruction of the Shtetl)

JESSY: Let's run away. I long for you and I can't bear the tyranny, not one moment longer. You should hear my father! They say –

ELI: Where to?

JESSY: Far.

ELI: How far? As far as Shklov? That isn't far enough from Suczorno. They have spies in Shklov.

JESSY: I didn't say Shklov, you did.

ELI: Alright, I did. Where else could you go? And how? On foot maybe or by a train, that comes or doesn't.

Sitting in railway stations, Russian style, for days to hear that Jews should walk if they want to live.

JESSY: My father said news from Lvov is, the Germans are everywhere in Poland. Jews and even Poles – would you believe – have swum the River Pruth down to the city of Czernovitz. It was just before Yom Kippur – the Day of Atonement. They come from everywhere – they swim the rivers. They sit in the open to pray. No bread, as this is a "fast" day. Eli, let's run away together. We'll be separated otherwise. I can't bear it.

ELI: Shklov is worse. At least here we still have a mother, fathers, brothers and sisters. People have ovens with wood in them . . .

JESSY: I did not mean Shklov. I meant let's run East. My older brother did. And my father said "go." My mother wrung her hands. We were sitting around the table and father says, "They will be here in a day or two. We do not know the direction they are taking. There is a war on. Go, my sons. Go East." He looks at me and starts crying. A father crying like an old woman. It breaks my heart. But I have no respect for tears. Then he turns to Mother and me and says, "You can't run anywhere. You stay with me and the Almighty will protect us." Why would he, I ask you, protect us, who can't help ourselves, women, old men?

ELI: I can't take you, Jessy. If I run, I go alone or go with my brothers. Or just wait it out. With you.

JESSY: I love you, Eli. I'll sneak out at night. When Suczorno is asleep. Being on the right side of the creek, the high bank – does our creek have a name?

ELI: It is too small to have a name. It's just there to divide us from the owners of your side of it, who collect rent from people like my father, a good man, who never made it, working for wages.

JESSY: He didn't work for my father.

ELI: No, he didn't. He worked for another rich man, clever enough to keep us barely alive, to haul his junk.

JESSY: I grew up on that side. People are good.

ELI: Some.

JESSY: My father is. Overbearing, tyrannical, yes. But he taught you a trade. You can fashion a window frame much better than he ever did.

ELI: Yes, he taught me.

JESSY: Why are you saying things against him? I have the right to because I love him. He always found a good word for me. When he went to Odessa for new tools, he bought me the best spun wool to knit. "For my angel," he said twice, "for my angel."

ELI: If he's so great, why run away from him? Stay.

JESSY: Let's not talk about fathers. I love you. At night I'll slip out. Our side of the creek is higher. A lovely high bank and you can see my window across the little bridge.

ELI: I don't promise. We'll see. Jessy, you're crazy. No good can come of it.

JESSY: We'll make plans, kiss and talk. There's no harm in love.

ELI: There is. In the eyes of Suczorno there is.

JESSY: I have money. All sorts of money. From my mother's mother. Ten Napoleons, all gold. Given to me, the only girl for generations. Not to share with anyone. Left to me. Give me your hand. Hold it a little longer. Don't take it away.

ELI: Stop it, Jessy. Give me my hand back.

JESSY: No, I won't. It is mine. Until you promise to come tonight.

Evening

A cool fragrant night. October. Earth in the air. Jessy looks around her silent house, brothers curled up, muddy shoes beside their bed. They're young. Loved and fed and made to study so early.

Last embers still visible. Jessy looks for her things. What to wear, what to take. She goes into the cupboard barefoot, takes the end piece of the Challah (bread) and puts it into a bag that she sewed herself. It was her first try on the Singer sewing machine, her mother's pride and joy. Jessy straightens the bag and smiles at her childhood caught in these seams. A few apples. She runs to the window, looks across between the bushes to see a dark shadow moving. A jump in her heartbeat. It's time. Hurry! Grabs dresses, whatever she finds. Rips the blanket – a light linen-type thing – from the bed. Folds the blanket around the apples. Looks about her. The window. Shuts it fast, bends down towards the drawers of her bed. Pulls open the small, precious, elegant one. Sees her wooden box, inlaid with Torah Scrolls. Jessy takes her gold dowry, throws the coins into her bag, and closes the drawer with a pain in her heart she has no time for. She straightens and leans against the door, facing her world one last time. Turns. Fears the noise of the key, but it moves in its lock as if oiled the day before. She slides out and rests against the closed door, watching the lower bank. A clear night, a half-moon. And now she wants to run across that bridge, to hide in Eli's arms, but waits to see him emerge. Eli seems taller at night, an enormous shadow turning him into an almost menacing figure. Her Eli. Different at night.

She follows the direction of his outstretched arm. Not inviting her to cross the bridge to him, telling her to walk east along her side of the bank. The high bank. Walking faster now, both separate on their side of the creek, closer to it, hoping the bushes will cover their shadows, until they both reach the end of the village. They cross the last bridge, clasp hands and continue to walk.

With the river in sight, a moon in it without a ripple, they pause to rest.

They are awakened by echoing shots, a gray smoke-laden sky, and the vision of their village in flames against the horizon.

THE GHOST TOWN OF KAZIMIERZ
From *Ghost Children*

by Lillian Boraks-Nemetz

A ghost town unravels
like a ball of gray wool disappearing
into sunlight as if it never was

people walk in silence
stepping in the footsteps
of those before them – footsteps
of the Hasidim silenced by Nazis

here is another market square
now dead but once alive
with the voices of women
men children and rabbis

the streets
unfold like the pages
of the Hebrew Bible:

The Street of Isaak
The Street of Josef
The Street of Jakob
The Street of Moses
The Street of Ester

here nothing has changed
except the people

VI

The Camps

SURVIVOR STORY:
Buchenwald

by Robbie Waisman

I was born in 1931 in Skarszysko, Poland, a very tight-knit community. I was the youngest of six children, with four older brothers and a sister. My parents were religious. I remember the Sabbath as a very special time when my father would tell us stories of the great rabbis and the stories of Sholom Aleichem. I was very pampered and felt that everything revolved around me. My early memories are full of warmth and love.

After Hitler's rise to power, I remember my parents' discussions. They were frightened and could not believe the situation that was developing around us. My father believed that Germany was too civilized to be capable of atrocities.

The Holocaust

I was eight years old in 1939 when my city was bombed and occupied by the Nazis. I thought that it was a game until I saw a man shot to death. I matured forty years in that instant. In 1940, the ghetto was formed. At this time my parents sent me to stay with a non-Jewish family. After three weeks I ran away and returned to my family in the ghetto. In 1941, my eldest brother, Chaim, heard that the ghetto was going to be liquidated. That night he smuggled me out. The next day, everyone in the ghetto was sent to Treblinka and gassed. My mother was among them.

Even though I was too young, I managed to work alongside my brothers in the ammunitions factory until I came down with typhoid fever. I was unconscious for about ten days and covered up and hidden so as to go unnoticed. My brother Abraham also contracted the disease but was discovered and shot.

After I was separated from my father and brothers I befriended Abe, who was a year older than I was. We remained together for the rest of the war. In 1944, when I was thirteen, we were sent to Buchenwald Concentration Camp and placed in a barrack with Polish, French and German political prisoners, who helped protect us.

Liberation

I was liberated from Buchenwald on April 11, 1945 at the age of fourteen. My immediate concern was to be reunited with my family. At that time I was not yet aware of the enormity of the Holocaust, or of the extent of our losses. The human mind doesn't accept some of these things. I knew that my brother Abraham had died and I suspected my father was also dead, but I still hoped to find the rest of my family. I had no idea that my mother had died in Treblinka. My sister, Leah, is the only one of my family who survived.

I had no idea that there were 430 children scattered throughout Buchenwald. I had thought that Abe and I were the only children there. We were housed in the former SS barracks, where we each had a bed and clean sheets. Doctors and nurses examined us and wrote down our stories.

Displaced Persons Camps

We all wanted to go home, but we remained in Buchenwald for about three months because there was nowhere else to go. The authorities had a hard time convincing us that we could not go home and that it would be dangerous to return to Poland, where returning Jews had been killed in pogroms. I could not understand why people, other than the Nazis, wanted to kill us.

A very powerful bond developed among the children. All we had was one another. Looking back I realize what a blessing it was that we were together. They were my family. It took us a while to realize that we could go outside the gates of Buchenwald. At first we didn't dare to leave the camp, but then we started to go on little excursions around Buchenwald. We really savored this newfound freedom.

We started searching for surviving relatives. We registered our history and pictures with the Red Cross for distribution. During the war, many of us had promised our elders that if we survived, we would tell the world about what had happened.

MASS GRAVES

by Sarah Klassen

You find them in places
like Timisoara, Auschwitz,
Babi Yar.

(How strangely these names ride
on your tongue, somewhere between
horror and delight.

Names of the dead
if they were known to you
would be unspeakable.)

In Belsen,
bones of the old
and young must be somehow

disposed of. Thrown together
under cold earth and lime, skulls
leg bones, clavicles of all kinds

fuse. Most years at Christmas
you'll find them covered
poorly with snow.

THE COUNTY OF BIRCHES

by Judith Kalman

> *Through a collection of stories, a second generation Hungarian child strings together bits and pieces of her parents' dark past. In 1956 they leave Hungary. Homeless and displaced, Dana and her family leave their country and set out on a journey to Canada, to find a home and sense of belonging.*

Channel Crossing

A small person in a kerchief on a jostling train, I hold fast to the windowsill as the train rocks me with its rhythm. I've absorbed the motion, so that after hours of gazing out the blurry window my own body sways and clacks at a mechanical rate. We're going. I don't dwell on the departure so much as our passage. Moving, going, on our way.

My father, beside me, has sunk into himself since we boarded in Budapest's Keleti Pályaudvar. I sense inertia gathering like a mass in his warm bulk. Occasionally a hand reaches out automatically to steady me, but my father doesn't seem to be moving like the rest of us; he's given himself over to conveyance.

Seated with us in the compartment, my mother rapidly reviews the names of those who came to see us off, remarking archly on absences. Where was Apu's colleague Mátyás? He couldn't wait to step into Apu's job with the ministry of agriculture, not even long enough to see him to the station? Old Agi's arthritic knees hadn't held her back from getting a good look at our relatives, although she had liked to complain piteously when she was mopping our floors. Poor thing, look at these biscuits Agi brought, dry as dust. My mother prattles while sorting the packets of foodstuffs that were pressed on her with embraces. She passes them along to Lili, who recites their labels in the fluting oratory style she learned at school. Lili's voice trills over cherry-filled bonbons. Apu lifts a hand, distractedly waving off my mother's chatter as though she misses the point entirely.

"Look, Apu, see the moo-cows?" I ask. But, although he pats my shoulder, I can tell he doesn't notice. Otherwise he'd identify their breed for me, sum up their condition in a glance.

The platform of the Keleti Pályaudvar had swarmed with our relatives and friends, most of them the post-war remains of Apu's large extended family. Blowing into his monogrammed handkerchief, he wouldn't look through the glass. His round face, at the best of times doleful, was shadowed under the brim of his fedora. His fleshy palm, my domain, failed to respond to my tugs: "Apu, *A-pu*, when will the train start?"

It vexes me when he drifts off into that other place from before the war, but he usually makes up for it, returning to me and Lili and placating us with a story he found there. I remember one of my favorites, starting like a once-upon-a-time:

"When I was a very little boy, just about your age, Danuska, not even four, I was taken for the first time to my beloved Great-Uncle Itzák's, to commemorate the *Yahrzeit* of his late father, your ancestor Hermann Grószmann. This was a grand occasion. Every year there came hundreds: relations, friends, rabbis, beggars from far and wide, for it was considered a blessing to give, especially to the poor. The more you would give in this world, the closer you would be to God in the next. And Great-Uncle Itzák was both a rich and a pious man.

"I was hardly more than a babe in arms, still with ringlets to my shoulders, but old enough to know that if I made a commotion my mother would not leave me behind. So, after a shameful display of willfulness that, I'm sorry to say, made my poor beloved father throw up his hands, he had the coachman put an extra fur rug into the *szánkó*, where, bundled in the back between my dear mother and father, I excitedly awaited the flick of the reins that would begin my first journey from the Rákóczi Tanya."

Who can resist the charm of horse-drawn sleighs and a father's childhood misbehavior? But I resent it when he stays locked in that place and won't come out, assailed by other kinds of memories that make him feel no good can come of our endeavors.

I have no patience with Apu when he doesn't see that the bad things are over. Especially when it is daytime and he is with me and Lili. Things are good now, his children safe beside him. Not like the time when he was made to enlist in the labor battalion, board the train at their private platform on the Rákóczi Tanya, and be borne away from his family estate. Each labor service Apu went through, he's said, he thought would be the end of him. Yet it was he who survived, those he left at home lost. Vicious joke of fate, he has spat into the night. What kind of joke is that, I wondered. Wife, daughter, niece; parents, brothers; cousins, aunts, uncles. One night, in a fit of remorseless self-punishment, I heard him count off

the kinfolk lost. All hauled away by the rails he now presumes
to ride into a better world.

Apu won't look at what he's leaving. The betraying grind
of the wheels holds him fast. He can't accept he is abandoning
all that remains of what he knew and loved. He is leaving yet
again but – *by choice* – the dear familiar faces. He wouldn't look
at them in the station despite my insistence on what was plain:
"Apu, see. See! Blanka-néni's waving."

Apu does not glance out the train window as we pass the
flat fields of the Hungarian countryside. He says no good-bye.
From the first jolt of the train as it prepared to groan out of the
Keleti Pályaudvar, Apu let go the reins. As the train jerked to a
start, he disengaged.

Despite my father's withdrawal, I let myself be mesmerized
by the flow of images on the window's changing screen. That
Apu is gloomy does not really matter. Parents *are* gloomy.
Gloomy and anxious and often irritable. It doesn't trouble me.
I know I'm central – Lili and I. We're a force that wrenches my
father from the past he cherishes. We little girls, me trained to
the window, Lili older but still charmed by store-bought pack-
ages, we small priestesses of motion are his transport. We were
invoked by my mother for months. She wanted a future for her
children. How was she to provide it when every penny he
made he spent on his aunts and cousins? Did he not see while
he fretted over the petty quarrels of the great-aunties that all
his reaching into his pockets wouldn't recover their losses?
She wasn't about to be sacrificed! Not she, nor anything of
hers. His first wife and child went up in smoke. Enough sacrificed. Not her. Not hers.

Lili and me. Hers. Her children. It is spring of 1957. Gunfire in Budapest during the fall revolution made her call up our names in the same breath as the future. We are going to a place where the future resides.

Apu pulls me down abruptly and holds me tight. He presses his face to mine, and his warm tears make our cheeks stick. It feels as though he's hanging on to me. Taken aback, I wonder with dawning alarm how I will manage to hold him up. My little arms wriggle and struggle free. They circle his neck like a life buoy, for I feel light and floatable and he is adrift.

Once we cross the Hungarian border there's no turning back. The passports, just exit visas really, only let us out. I deduce this from the way Apu concedes authority to my mother. In Hungary he was a patriarch to his family. He had a position of repute in his field. He was at home and in command of his milieu. On the train he can't even speak. Some internal inflexibility keeps him from testing new sounds. Apu lacks my mother's fluidity with language. She tries out foreign words on any train official who passes us. When she gets a response, however incomprehensible, her mouth sets in a satisfied line.

Lili's head rocks in my mother's lap. When I tear my eyes from the window, I glimpse Lili's big hair bow drooping atop her head like a giant butterfly with folded wings. I wish I could wear my hair like Lili's, but it is too fine to hold such an ornament.

Unlike Lili, I resist sleep and try to keep my eyes open. I think that by staying watchful I can prevent anything bad from taking place. Really I trust the worst is over, but it's smart to be prepared. If need be, Lili and I can benefit from the tragic mistakes of the past. *We* will know who to call, when to get out, where to run to, how to live.

Our half-sister, Clárika, as I've seen her in a photograph Apu keeps wrapped in his prayer shawl, was a serious child, bird-boned, with straight hair tied up in a fat ribbon like Lili's. But while Lili's mouth is full and usually animated, our half-sister looks pinched and studious, older than her six years. Beside her stands her cousin, who was raised with her on the Tanya. They look like mismatched twins. They're the same height, but the cousin's face is round and impish, with the same screwed-up little grin I wear in the passport photo taken before we left. It is the grin of the great-aunties and, Apu says, of his mother.

I don't imagine my grandmother with a screwed-up impish grin. I see her always on a death train, chanting a low prayer. She fingers something fine and beautiful as she prays. Mari-néni, one of the relatives who came back, said my grandmother was stopped before boarding the train by someone called Eichmann. There is always silence when that name is uttered. *Eichmann.* I cringe from whispering it even to myself.

"*Was ist das?*" Eichmann had demanded, holding up the white silk shawl my grandmother always wore on Yom Kippur. Mari-néni said my grandmother looked past the monster as though he were just a post and answered flatly, not in German, but in the Yiddish she knew he'd understand: "Clothes to die in." Mari-néni brought these words back to Apu like a keepsake.

She recalled too how my half-sister had held tightly to her mother's hand all that final journey. Her mother's gentle voice never faltered, calmly reassuring, "Soon we'll catch up with

Apu. Soon we'll join your father." I imagine the pinched, serious child's face but can't hold it in my mind for long. It slides, instead, into the visage of the other, the little cousin with the wrinkle-nosed grin and abundant curls that might have saved the two children.

"The Rákóczi Tanya where I grew up was a big estate with many holds of land that we farmed for tobacco," Apu has told us. "It was the largest tobacco plantation in Hungary, but the estate itself was small compared to the lands next to ours, belonging to the Gyorgyi counts. On the counts' land there were two castles, no less. The eldest count, Count László, occupied the big *kastély* for part of the year, but no one in his family used the smaller manor house. The little kastély, as it happened, was located beside the Rákóczi Tanya, and one day, if you can believe, the count called for my father and offered to lease him the little kastély for our use. Jews in a kastély, can you imagine? Well, as it turned out, your beloved and devout grandmother could not. She told my father to graciously decline the offer. Appealing as it might have been for me and my young brothers to live in a castle, our mother would not dream of making a kosher household out of a place that had housed generations of Catholic aristocrats."

To pass up the chance of living in a castle, how I regret it! But my father sounded proud of his mother's response, as though she meant that the castle was not actually good enough for them.

Later Apu would have occasion to reject a proposal of the younger count's. Catching sight of the two little Jewish girls during the last months of the war, Count Ernö felt moved by the pretty cousin's typical Magyar beauty to make an offer.

Let the girls come to him to be raised as his own. Come what may, he would do what he could for them.

Oh, I think hopefully, even though I know the real end of the story, I see that it doesn't have to end so badly after all. The children, the little children, as is right and proper and fair, at least the children could be saved!

"Let them go!" Apu wrote back to his wife in a letter from his last posting in the labor service. He was furious. What kind of proposal was Count Ernö making? How could the count allow himself to take advantage of the vulnerability of the children's mothers, while Apu and his brother Miki were away in service? It was a scandal, the very idea, to split up the family and abandon the children among strangers, *gentiles*. What assurances would there be for their safety? What was the matter with Miri? Was she so lacking in natural feeling that she could actually entertain such a notion? Under no circumstances should they let their child – or the other – go!

Not even one? I beg in my head, as I hear the bitter ending. Not even the pretty one with the impish grin? At least her, the one the count liked best?

According to Mari-néni, not once on the hellish journey had my half-sister's mother relinquished the little hand. Seared into mind as though I had seem them myself are mother and child, stripped naked, still clasped together under the spigots for gas.

The train, while it's moving, is safe, but when it stops I spin, panicked. I vibrate from the steel that whirs inside me. Though the train stops, I continue.

"Here we are!" declares my mother.

"What! Where are we going? What are you doing?" I gasp as she stuffs our scattered belongings into her satchel.

"It's Bécs, see, Wien – Vienna. We change here."

Change?

What change? Isn't it supposed to be days before we arrive at our destination? I can't stand being herded without explanation. I hate not knowing what to expect.

"Hurry," says my mother, bustling Lili into her overcoat.

There are so many bundles I can tell she'll forget something. Food, coats, blankets, papers. She seems distracted. Apu is already on the platform, weighed down by the brown metal trunk and our three leather valises. He is stuck with the valuables, the photographs of people I shall never meet, and all the crumpled, mud-stained letters he wrapped in a white, gold-threaded prayer shawl and packed away tenderly. We are supposed to have with us only what is most essential for travel, what we can actually carry, and he has brought the dead.

I am suddenly afraid for my father down there, separated from us and encumbered by that cargo. He can't forgive himself the harsh words he wrote to his wife. In punishment, I have heard him tell that story over and over again. I wish he would believe that it wasn't his fault. He had no choice when he was sent off in the labor battalion. And he couldn't have saved them anyway. He didn't know they would die. It was almost the end of the war. He has said himself that when he boarded the train for that last labor service, he felt as close to light of heart as the times permitted. The war was almost over. The Russians were outside their borders. So far, Hungary had escaped German occupation. But the Germans entered anyway and, in a flash, the person called Eichmann swept all the Jews out of the Hungarian countryside. Apu has said a number. Half a million Hungarian Jews gone in two weeks. That doesn't mean anything really, until I count his dear ones among them. How can he think that unforgivably, blindly, *he* was responsible?

I rehearse the list of our baggage obsessively, maddening my mother.

"Yes, yes. We have everything, don't worry."

But she doesn't pay enough attention, I think. She fails to catalogue what she stuffs away. Snatching up this or that and making it carelessly disappear. Someone must be vigilant, make sure nothing is left behind.

I can't digest what happened, that in a fleeting moment of time, everything was irrevocably lost. I struggle against that ephemeral instant, but it prevails. The brief but endless journey is my emotional locus, fixed. Apu's first wife and small daughter barely stepped into Auschwitz and were gone in a flash. Lili and I are so lucky. Lucky. Lucky. We were blessed with luck to have been born after all that.

"Apu," I shout, throwing myself from the narrow opening of the train, straight over the rattling steps into his quick arms.

ALL THERE IS TO KNOW ABOUT
ADOLPH EICHMANN

by Leonard Cohen

EYES: .... Medium
HAIR: .... Medium
WEIGHT: .... Medium
HEIGHT: .... Medium
DISTINGUISHING FEATURES: .... None
NUMBER OF FINGERS: .... Ten
NUMBER OF TOES: .... Ten
INTELLIGENCE: .... Medium

What did you expect?

Talons?

Oversize incisors?

Green saliva?

Madness?

SURVIVOR STATEMENT

PETER SUEDFELD

I was born in Budapest, Hungary in 1935. In 1944, when the Germans occupied Hungary, my mother was deported to Auschwitz, where she perished. Most of my family was sent to labor battalions, concentration camps, or the ghetto. During the siege of Budapest, using a false name and Catholic papers, I was hidden in various places by an International Red Cross orphanage. The orphanage was bombed during the Russian air raid on Budapest. I became one of the cellar children, moving repeatedly from one cellar of a bombed building to another. I had to scrounge for food in the backyards and ruins of burnt buildings.

VII

Resistance

SURVIVOR STATEMENT

BENTE NATHAN THOMSEN

I was born in Copenhagen, Denmark in 1935. I will never forget April 9, 1940, when the sky over our city was filled with the drone of German airplanes. Three years later we learned that all the Jewish people were to be deported. My father assured me that we would go to Sweden, a neutral country that provided a safe haven for Jews and other displaced persons. Late on the night of October 2, 1943, we crawled along a water-filled ditch to the sea, where we boarded a small fishing boat and crossed safely into Sweden. In June 1945 we were able to return home to Denmark.

LISA

by Carol Matas

*Denmark is overrun by the Nazis,
but resistance springs up against the
oppressors. Lisa's Jewish family is
deeply implicated in trying to help
save other Jews. Lisa persuades
her parents that even though she
is still in school, she too can make
a difference.*

Chapter Three
Stefan and Jesper

I'm sitting in class, trying not to stare at the clock, waiting for the school day to be over. I have a plan. I'm going to follow Stefan today.

I know he's up to something. I overheard him and Jesper having a big fight two nights ago. Mother and Father were out; the boys were sitting at the kitchen table. My door was open a crack, and I could hear perfectly. Eavesdropping is starting to become a habit.

Jesper said, "Look, my contact says that the resistance doesn't want Jewish people in dangerous situations, situations where they can be caught. The Germans will only use that as an excuse. 'See, here we have Jewish saboteurs. Now you see why we have to round up the Jews and send them away. They threaten the very peace of Denmark.'"

"So you want me to just sit here and do nothing?" Stefan growled.

"Not me, Stefan, the resistance – and some of them are Jewish. They don't want to take any more chances than necessary. But they need people for the underground printing presses. You could do that."

"So the Jews are supposed to keep quiet and not make trouble?" Stefan objected. "That did them a lot of good in Germany." I could hear him push back his chair; he paced the room. "Don't you see, Jesper? There *is* trouble. We're not making it; we're trying to help unmake it. No, it's up to us to fight, any way we can. There will be lots of people for the presses – not so many for the other work. And if you have to lie to your superiors, lie. Or just don't tell them I'm Jewish. I don't care. But I'm going to work along with you."

Jesper sighed. "You're right," he said. "I agree with you. If the Germans want an excuse to round up the Jews, they'll make one up. They don't need real evidence." Jesper had pushed his chair back, too. "I'll talk to them, Stefan. I'll tell them it's both of us or neither of us. I'm not going to lie. I'll make them listen."

After that I started thinking and I realized that, in fact, everyone in my house was acting strangely. But no one admits to a thing. Father stays out until all hours. I know because I wait up, just to be sure he gets home all right. I stare into the dark until I hear the outside door open and close softly. And Mother, well, she seems to be doing her regular things – going to the university to teach English, always back by the time I'm home from school – but I don't know, I have this feeling. . . .

It's been over six months since the Germans came. They're everywhere. On every city block there are pairs of them out on patrol, or rows and rows of them parading down the street. Sometimes, when there are just two of them, Stefan and I play chicken. We walk straight for them, talking, pretending not to notice them, and see who moves aside first. Often they do, but sometimes they don't, and then I think Stefan carries it too far. He'll walk right between them. Once one of them hit him, right in the side, with the butt of his rifle. That didn't stop Stefan; it just made him more determined. But with SS men or the Gestapo, even Stefan doesn't play chicken.

I'm almost thirteen now, and I want to do something. Playing chicken is just not enough. I'm not stupid; I know people are doing things. Sometimes I find leaflets on the streetcars, telling the news from the war – the real news about what's going on. One I read described how Norway fought the Germans, really fought, and destroyed a huge part of Germany's navy. So even though Norway ended up occupied, just like us, they made a big difference in the war and really helped the Allies. Another leaflet described how three factories were blown up right here in Copenhagen, factories that made things such as boots and radio parts that helped the Germans. And another was all jokes and cartoons about the Germans. I'll bet they hate that the worst – being laughed at.

Someone must be printing the leaflets, getting them out. I asked Stefan, but he said I'm too young and I'm a girl. Well, I'm as big as he is – bigger, actually – and he's lucky I didn't flatten him. I could, but I don't, out of pity. And, of course, there's the small chance that he's stronger than he looks. He can be pretty fierce when he gets mad.

At last, the school bell. I've got to get out of here before Stefan leaves his school in the building next door. I run out just in time to see Stefan and Jesper turn the corner in the direction of Østerbrogade. At first it's easy to follow them because there are so many other kids on the street. I just stay behind the crowd. But after a while most have gone home and the streets are getting empty. Now it's only them, me, and a couple of others walking. If Stefan and Jesper turn, they're sure to see me. They seem to be heading toward the children's playground. I decide to take a chance and get there another way.

I turn down Classensgade and end up in the playground. I hide behind a tree and see them coming the other way. They're looking around now, really casually, but I can tell they're checking to see if anyone is around. A man is walking in from Stokvej. He has a big coat on. It's November, and damp and cloudy and pretty cool, but he's dressed for winter. He sits down on a bench. When he gets up, he's left a large package behind. Jesper and Stefan sit down on either side of the package. I notice they're wearing their long winter coats, too. They're doing something, shoveling the contents of the package inside their coats. Now they're walking away. They're heading out of the park. They walk practically right past me, back to Østerbrogade, and wait for the streetcar. They get on.

What should I do? They'll see me if I get on, but if I don't I'll lose them. I decide to make a run for it. But I'm too late – the streetcar moves away and I'm left standing there. I can see Stefan looking at me through a window, his face all crinkled up and worried.

I realize that if I run really fast and cut through the park, I may be able to catch the streetcar two stops ahead. I've got very long legs, and when I want to run I can really move. I get to the stop, panting, a biting pain in my side, about half a minute before the streetcar. I try to look really calm as I get on and sit down. I look around for Stefan, but I can't see him. Then there's a tap on my window, and he and Jesper wave to me from outside as the streetcar moves away. They're laughing. I jump up and start to call Stefan the worst, the dirtiest name I can think of – when I notice everyone is looking at me. I sit down. A freedom fighter has to learn control. So I bite my nails.

Then I see it. On the floor. A small piece of folded paper. I'm sitting alone in my seat. I look across the aisle; no one is looking at me. I reach down slowly, pick up the piece of paper, slip it in my pocket. Then I get off the streetcar at the next stop.

I'm about eight blocks from home now. I hurry. The paper feels as though it's burning in my pocket. I reach our building, throw open the door, slip across the waxed foyer floor, then take the steps two at a time. I rush into the apartment and into my room, slamming both doors. My mother calls to me from the kitchen, "Lisa, is that you? You're late." I open the note. Yes, it's a bulletin from the resistance. They've managed to blow up a tool factory and some rail lines. They tell us to listen to Radio Free Denmark for more information.

"Lisa?" My mother knocks. I crumple the paper and stuff it in my pocket. I know how it got into the streetcar.

"Lisa, may I come in?"

"Yes, Mother."

She opens the door.

"Lisa," she says, "where were you?"

"Nowhere," I answer. "Just walking."

"Were you with a friend?"

"No."

"Lisa, I want you straight home or I want to know where you are. Otherwise I worry."

"Yes, Mother."

She closes the door. I throw off my jacket and plop down on my bed. One more problem I hadn't thought of. She'll want to know where I am every minute. I'll just have to start making up excuses, like going to Susanne's or something. I wait impatiently for Stefan to get home. He's always home for supper so he can listen to the radio later. I'll have to convince him to let me help.

MY CANARY YELLOW STAR

by Eva Wiseman

1944. The Nazis reach Hungary and march into Budapest. One night Hungarian fascist troops – the Arrow Cross – storm into the Weisz family's apartment in a designated "Jewish building." Marta's grandmother is murdered, the house sealed, the family close to starvation. Can they enlist Wallenberg's help? Raoul Wallenberg rescued one hundred thousand Hungarian Jews from death during the Holocaust.

Chapter Eleven
Mr. Wallenberg

This time when we lined up in the courtyard, there were fewer of us. The faces around me were more haggard and much thinner than before. We had remembered the bone-chilling cold from the last time the Arrow Cross had descended upon us, so now everybody had put on winter clothing even though it was four o'clock in the morning and we'd been given only a few minutes to get dressed. I also remembered to put my Schutz-Pass in my pocket. Judit had even thrown a winter blanket over her coat for extra warmth, but in her haste, she had forgotten to pull on her shoes. She hopped up and down in one spot to keep her feet from freezing in the flimsy bedroom slippers she was wearing.

The younger women and children were quickly separated from the rest of the group and marched out of the courtyard at gunpoint. There were no goodbyes. The Arrow Cross guards prodded us with the muzzles of their guns while Judit and I clung together in a futile attempt at protection. Despite the men's threats, our progress was slow. If anyone stopped or even paused, a deafening shot rang out. We learned to step over the bodies and keep moving. We had no choice. The streets were littered with hundreds of corpses whose faces were covered with sheets of newspaper. I wondered if I knew any of the victims. Could Ervin and Gabor and Adam be among those lying on the ground? I looked and looked with morbid curiosity. I couldn't help myself.

The long march continued. At least a hundred more young women and children joined us at different points. The rays of the rising sun escaped the glowering clouds like punctuation marks, emphasizing the desperation on our faces. We finally stopped at the foot of the Chain Bridge, spanning the Danube River. By then, choking fear had gripped my hands, my belly, and my feet. Several people on their way to work had gathered around our group, chatting, laughing, pointing fingers in our direction. One fat old woman in a black babushka broke away from the crowd and walked up to Judit. Without looking into her face or acknowledging her existence with a glance or a word, she grabbed the blanket off Judit's shoulders, turned on her heels, and walked away with it. Judit stood staring after her with an open mouth. I squeezed her arm.

"Don't say anything! Pretend nothing happened."

"But I . . ."

Her voice trailed off as two of the Arrow Cross brutes dragged a young mother and her twin sons to the front of the crowd. One of the little boys was crying and the other sucked his thumb. Both were clinging to their mother, who tried to shield them with her arms. The guards tied a thick rope around the waist of each of the little boys, then wound it around the waist of their protesting mother. They next bound the mother's feet with a heavy metal chain. Using the barrels of their guns, they shoved the pathetic trio to the very edge of the Danube. Three of the Arrow Cross guards then lined up in a straight line and pointed their guns at the distraught mother and the frightened children. She covered her boys' eyes with her hands just before a loud shot rang out. Blood spurted out of the mother's mouth as she catapulted into the murky river, dragging her screeching little sons after her. The bubbles on the turgid waters were soon erased by angry waves. A gray seagull looked on for a moment, then lost interest, flapped its dirty wings, and was gone. Everything was so quiet that the sudden collective intake of breath of the Jewish captives could clearly be heard. Suddenly, the loud clapping of the onlookers broke the silence. The skies wept in sympathy.

We marched at gunpoint in the pelting rain for hours. We were soaked to the skin, and Judit's plaid bedroom slippers were in tatters. Finally, we arrived at a cavernous brick factory on the Buda side of the river. Our guards led us into a dark warehouse used to dry bricks. The huge space was dimly lit by a few grimy windows near the ceiling. I tried to get my bearings, but it was too dark to see. Slowly, I was able to make out what seemed to be hundreds and hundreds of bodies lying on the floor or leaning against the walls. Suddenly, I tripped and fell. My leg was caught in a deep hole. Judit yanked me out with all her might. As my eyes became accustomed to the semi-darkness, I saw that the entire floor was dotted with air vents like the one I had stepped into. Those who lost their footing in these holes were in danger of being trampled by the surging crowd.

We pushed our way to a corner of the vast room. Brick dust covered the walls and even the ceiling. It stuck to our clothes, giving us a ghostly appearance, made our eyes sting, and got into our noses and our mouths, making it hard to breathe.

"I feel as if I'm under water, as if I'm choking," Judit said.

"Me too! I'm afraid I'll throw up."

My stomach grumbled, but there was no water or food. When anyone asked to go to the washroom, a rifle butt or a kick by a polished boot signaled a quick refusal. Before long, the stench of urine mixed with the smell of stale sweat made my stomach turn over.

The hours dragged by. Judit and I huddled together, holding hands. I must have dozed off on the hard floor, for a sudden, loud clanging startled me. I looked around and saw that the wide steel gates leading into the warehouse were being pushed open. A dozen figures were silhouetted against the outside brightness. I shaded my eyes to see them.

The sea of prisoners parted in front of a slightly built man with an air of quiet authority. He was dressed in a long, black coat, gray fedora, and hiking boots. He was carrying a brown rucksack in his right hand. It was the man we'd met in Percel Street. Close behind him was a burlier companion, similarly dressed. The second man was carrying a large megaphone under his arm. They were surrounded by eight armed Arrow Cross guards. The group stopped in the middle of the crowd, and the cavernous room grew still.

"I am Raoul Wallenberg from the Swedish embassy," announced the first man through the megaphone. He was speaking in a heavily accented but easily understood Hungarian. "I am here to identify all Swedish citizens. Those of you with a Schutz-Pass in your possession will be released immediately."

I patted my coat pocket. The bulge made by the document was comforting under my fingers, but Judit's sudden intake of breath reminded me that she didn't have any Swedish papers. A desperate murmur broke out in the crowd.

"What about the rest of us?" an old woman cried.

"Please help my child! Please help my baby!" begged a wild-eyed young woman in a tweed coat. She held her baby in Wallenberg's direction.

The noise of the crowd grew louder. I saw an Arrow Cross guard smile and make slicing motions across his throat. Wallenberg waved his hands for quiet. His face was a study in sorrow.

"I am very sorry, but I can't help the rest of you. I have no authority," he said in a quiet voice. "But I do have the authority to acquire the immediate release of all Swedish subjects," he added firmly. "All Swedish citizens, anybody with a Schutz-Pass, please line up along that wall." He pointed to the far end of the room. Only then did I notice that a long wooden table and two chairs had been set up under the grimy windows. Wallenberg and his companion walked over to the table and sat down. The Swede opened up his rucksack and took out a black ledger and a fountain pen.

Those with Schutz-Passes separated from the rest of the crowd and began to form a line.

"You'd better go and line up with them," Judit said, trying to smile through her tears. "Let me give you a hug for good luck!"

Someone behind me jostled me. I lurched forward, stepping on my friend's foot.

"Ouch!"

"Sorry!"

"Not your fault," Judit said. "These slippers aren't good for much." Her toes showed through the ragged material. We looked at each other for a long moment. The lack of good shoes meant frozen toes, and the inability to walk meant almost certain death. If a prisoner could not keep up with the crowd, the Arrow Cross would shoot the poor wretch. I began to cry and Judit knew why.

"Don't worry about me! I'll be fine." She forced a smile and patted my arm. "Maybe I'll be lucky and they won't make us walk very far."

"No chance of that!" We had both heard rumors of the Arrow Cross forcing their Jewish captives to march long distances under gunpoint until they were ready to drop. Only the fittest won the dubious prize of being handed over to the German authorities.

"I wish my shoes would fit you," I exclaimed in frustration.

"Well, they won't. Not these boats," Judit said. "It's my own fault – I should have remembered my shoes. But don't worry! I'll be fine."

Before I could think, I reached into my pocket and took out the billfold that contained my Schutz-Pass. In the chaos surrounding us, nobody was paying attention as I slipped it into Judit's hand.

"Here! The picture on it is so grainy that nobody will be able to tell it isn't of you," I told her. "Everybody says we look alike."

"Marta, I couldn't!" Judit tried to return the billfold.

I pushed her hand away. "You have to. There's no other way. You won't survive a day's march without proper shoes. At least I have shoes I can walk in."

Judit opened and closed her mouth, but no sound came out. We both knew I was right. I gave her a little shove in the direction of the long column of people waiting to see Wallenberg. Judit nodded reluctantly, handed me her own papers, and hugged me tightly before she was swallowed up by the crowd straining to reach the table against the wall.

I made my way back to the corner where we had been sitting and lowered myself onto my haunches. But I felt lonely, so I stood up again and pushed my way through the crowd, desperate to find someone, anyone familiar. I thought I saw Mrs. Lazar across the huge room and tried to make my way toward her. By the time I crossed the sea of humanity, however, she had disappeared and I found myself at the very back of the throng waiting to see Wallenberg. I stayed where I was. The long line moved at a brisk pace, and I moved along with it. The closer and closer I got to the front, to the Swede sitting at the table, the more panicky I became. If I left the line, I would be deported. If I stayed in the line, I would still be deported since I didn't have my pass. It wasn't until the very moment I reached the front of the line that I knew what had to be done. One of the Arrow Cross youths guarding Wallenberg butted me in the back with the barrel of his rifle to make me move closer. I stumbled and had to grip the edge of the table to prevent myself from falling on top of it.

"Put down your rifle," Wallenberg said to the guard in a quiet, authoritative voice. "Put that gun down immediately."

To my surprise, the guard lowered his weapon with a sheepish expression on his face. After giving the guard a long, cold look, Wallenberg turned his attention to me. His face relaxed into a smile. "I believe we've met before," he said politely. "May I see your Schutz-Pass, please?"

I could only gape at him.

"Your Schutz-Pass, please," he repeated patiently.

"I lost my Schutz-Pass on the way here," I managed to croak. "It was in my pocketbook. One of the Arrow Cross took it away from me back at our apartment house when they rounded us up."

"Lying Jew!" cried the soldier standing next to the table. He lifted his rifle into the air, ready to smash it down on my head. I lifted my hands to cover my face and began to pray under my breath. The blow did not fall.

"Stop or I'll report you to your superiors!" thundered Wallenberg. "I demand you put down your gun!"

To my surprise, for the second time, the guard obeyed.

Wallenberg turned back to me. "It's unfortunate you lost your papers, but I'm certain that we have a record of you in my ledger. We keep track of all of our Swedish subjects. What is your name, please?"

I suddenly realized that I couldn't tell him my name. Judit had already used my Schutz-Pass. There was no sign of her, so I was quite certain she had already been released. I tried to

think of another name to use, but in my panic I came up blank.
There were only two names in the whole, wide world that I
could remember – Judit's and mine.

"I am Judit Grof," I whispered.

"Judit Grof . . . Let me see," Wallenberg said. He turned a
few pages in his ledger and ran his finger down the page.

I had to remind myself to breathe.

"Judit Grof . . . Yes, here you are. Right between Izsak
Funk and Eszter Gross," he said pleasantly. "Please join
the others." He pointed to a large group being led toward the
open gates by three Arrow Cross guards. Three others were
silhouetted in the doorway against the sunny sky.

"Where is this girl's name? Show me her name in your
ledger! I don't believe she is in your book! The girl is a liar!"
The guard reached for Wallenberg's ledger. The Swede
slammed his book shut.

"How dare you question me?" he said coldly. "How dare
you! This girl is a Swedish subject. She is no concern of yours!
She is one of my Jews. I will report your behavior to your
commandant!"

The guard hesitated for an instant before turning his back
on us. "To hell with you both!" he muttered. "Who cares
about a lying Jew!"

"Hurry up, girl, or your group will be gone," Wallenberg
said.

"Thank you! Thank you very much," I mouthed to him.

I ran toward the exit. The armed guards in the doorway
stepped aside, and the sunshine blinded me.

A TIME TO CHOOSE

by Martha Attema

It's 1944 in the Nazi-occupied Netherlands. Sixteen-year-old Johannes has a conflict. He loves his parents, but is torn between his father's political affiliations and his own love and loyalty for Holland. How can the young man overcome this struggle and help his country?

The Plan

By late fall most people had given up hope for a quick liberation. December brought more cold weather to a country that had few resources left for heating. Electricity had been cut off due to a shortage of coal. The pumping stations were all out of order, so water levels rose and large areas became flooded. Food became extremely scarce, especially in the big cities. An endless stream of hungry people knocked on the farm door every day.

Some traded soap or jewelry for food. Others had nothing left to trade. To the annoyance of his father, Johannes' mother tried to give butter and milk to everybody who came to their door. Father was afraid he couldn't deliver enough milk to the Germans. Mother ignored his complaints.

With more frequency the Germans seized cattle for their troops and the people in Germany. Johannes' father organized the transportation of those cattle. Sometimes cows from other farmers were boarded at the van der Meer farm for a couple of days before being sent off. Since the argument a few weeks ago, his mother never mentioned the cows anymore. Johannes and Sietske also brought food to Johannes' grandparents in the village and to Grandmother van der Meer in Leeuwarden. They'd had no further trouble with German soldiers.

With no electricity and just the one carbide lamp, the evenings were long and boring. Johannes often played board games with Anneke, but his thoughts were elsewhere. He hadn't had too many assignments.

Two weeks before, an attack on the registration office at a neighboring municipality had been successful. During the night the resistance had walked in, taken food coupons and identity cards and destroyed all the registration cards of the people in the municipality. That wasn't the only raid on registration offices. With so many people in hiding, there was an urgent need for food coupons and identity cards. As a result, all municipal buildings and registration offices now had security guards twenty-four hours a day.

Johannes had not been part of that action. He's learned about it the next day from Sietske. Sietske's brothers were involved, and probably Minne as well. It was obvious the jobs he was allowed to do were minor and without risk. Were they just to keep him happy? The real work was done by members of the resistance who didn't have a father who was a member of the party. Minne worked at the Dijkstra farm to be close to where the resistance actions were organized.

Two weeks before Christmas, Mother announced, "Grand-mother and Grandfather de Boer are moving in to save firewood. It's better that they live here for the winter."

"Where will they stay?" Anneke asked. She worried about giving up her room.

"They can sleep in the front room. We never use it anyway. We'll move the double bed down from the attic. It's only for a little while. When the cold weather is over, they'll move back to their own house."

Johannes thought about his grandparents. He didn't mind his grandmother so much. She was a quiet person, but Grandfather liked to know everything they did. Hopefully, he wouldn't be too nosy. Johannes liked going his own way, especially now, when he was more involved with Sietske and the resistance.

Two days later his grandparents arrived. Johannes had to bike into the village to help them pack the few belongings they were to bring. They each had a suitcase tied to the back of their bicycles. In his saddlebags, Johannes carried jars with preserved vegetables from his grandparents' summer garden. The wind was biting cold and his grandfather had insisted they wear newspapers under their sweaters. Johannes didn't really want to, but once outside, it was making a difference.

"I'll bike at the front!" Grandfather called. "Grandmother follows me and you have the tail end, Johannes. You young people speed too much for us."

Johannes nodded and took his place at the rear. A tall, skinny man with gray, curly hair, Grandfather de Boer sat straight up on his bike. Behind him followed Grandmother.

She was short, her shoulders bent. She suffered from arthritis and her hands had become deformed over the years. Her thin, white hair was tied in a bun and covered with a woolen scarf.

They pedaled over the country roads. Every now and then Grandfather would point to a farm and yell something over his shoulder to Grandmother. On the main road they met many people in search of food. Once they passed a group of children without coats or sweaters, and Johannes saw his grandmother brush tears from her face.

When they arrived at the farm, Mother made substitute coffee and baked some wheat cookies that didn't really taste like anything. Anneke busied herself by helping her grandparents unpack. Grandfather quickly changed into his old work clothes and was ready to help with the milking.

Johannes went to the hayloft to feed the cows. Then he settled into his routine of milking. Just before he finished the second last cow, someone tapped him on the shoulder. Startled, he looked up. It was Sietske. He hadn't heard her enter the stable. She placed her hand on his arm.

"Can you come to the farm tonight at seven?" she whispered.

"Okay," he nodded. "I'll be there." Sietske disappeared as quickly as she had come. He hoped nobody had seen her so he didn't have to explain. Fortunately, since the night his father had lost his temper, he rarely questioned Johannes' comings and goings.

"Who was the pretty young lady sneaking up on you, Johannes?" His grandfather stood right beside him.

Johannes felt his cheeks burn. "It's Sietske from across the bridge. You have met her before, Grandfather."

"Sietske, the little girl who used to race with you on your bikes?" Grandfather asked.

"Yes, that's her."

"She's quite a young lady, Johannes. But why did she sneak up on you like that?"

Johannes sighed. "She is busy helping on their farm, so she didn't have much time, but she wants me to come over tonight." He hoped that would stop the interrogation.

"I don't think you should go out at night, Johannes. The police are becoming really strict after curfew."

"They won't see me, Grandfather," Johannes said. "I don't take the road. I walk though the meadow, cross the bridge and jump the ditch to Dijkstras' farmland."

"Give me the pail, Johannes." Grandfather reached out to take the milk pail from him. "I'd better talk to your father about this. I don't want you to go out."

Johannes walked away to feed the calves. He wished the old man would mind his own business. He wasn't going to stay home for him. Tonight might be important.

During supper that night, the conversation took a wrong turn. Grandfather's voice rose as he said, "That boy has too much freedom. He's only sixteen."

Father nodded and continued to eat.

Mother said, "These are different times than when we grew up, Father. There's nothing for the young people. They can't go out. Dances and parties are forbidden, so what can they do other than visit each other when they get a chance?"

Johannes quickly ate his bread and silently thanked his mother for the speech. She looked up from her plate, her face blank, then winked at him.

Johannes rose from the table. "Don't wait up for me and don't worry about me being seen. I have found the perfect place where I can quickly cross the bridge."

Grandfather's mouth formed a straight, thin line and he frowned under his bushy eyebrows. His father's face showed no emotion. Though her expression was blank, Mother's eyes were smiling.

Johannes hurried over to Sietske's farm and knocked three times on the kitchen window. Sietske opened the door and hugged him quickly. Then she pulled him inside. The kitchen seemed darker than before. The carbide lamp, which normally stood on the table, was gone. Two bicycles fastened on wooden blocks stood on each side of the table. Both bikes were occupied, one by Klaas, the other by Bauke. They were pedaling to keep the lights burning. It was their only source of light tonight.

"We ran out of carbide," Sietske explained. "Tomorrow we'll get more."

"Are you in good shape, Johannes?" Bauke asked. "We have to take turns tonight. We each bike for a half-hour."

"Sure," Johannes said. He looked around the table. Besides Sietske's parents and brothers, there were Minne and another young man. Johannes guessed he was probably in his early twenties. His face was skinny, with prominent cheekbones and a pointed chin. Next to him sat an older man, in his late forties or early fifties. His grayish-black hair was unkempt and he hadn't shaved for several days. He wore a navy-blue woolen sweater that was ripped at the neck. Johannes saw no sign of the Jewish family.

"Johannes, this is Willem," Sietske's father pointed to the older man, "and beside him is Jan."

Johannes nodded at both men.

"Sit down. We have to discuss the raid at the distribution office in the village to obtain more food coupons," Bauke said. "This province has become a haven for 'divers' – people in hiding. Since the *Arbeitseinsatz* (forced slave labor), the deportation of Jews, the railroad strike and the closing of the universities, we have had to hide and feed thousands of people."

"Don't forget the American, British and Canadian pilots who have been shot down and rescued," his brother added.

Bauke nodded in agreement. "We hide many Jewish families and downed pilots, as well as students, doctors and lawyers who don't cooperate with the Germans. And since last month, every man between seventeen and fifty-five who doesn't want to work in Germany needs food, a place to stay and a false identity card." He stopped biking and the light in the room turned dim.

Minne took over, and Bauke sat down at the table in Minne's place. He wiped his forehead with the sleeve of his patched, flannel shirt. "Several families in the area are hiding people, and there are not enough food coupons being distributed every month to feed the extra mouths." He looked around the circle of people.

Johannes felt his heart beat faster. Good. Now he was being asked to do some real stuff. Johannes glanced up at Minne. Was that mockery in his old friend's eyes, or was it his imagination?

"This is my plan." Bauke looked around the circle. "Many raids on distribution offices have been successful."

"Not all, Bauke," Willem interrupted, his voice heavy. "The one from last week was discovered. The security police threw seven of our members in jail."

Bauke cleared his throat. "I know, Willem. But we are not here to discuss the actions that go wrong. Tomorrow night before curfew, we'll raid our municipality office. Two at a time, we'll travel to the village. At seven o'clock some of you will meet at the back of the local office. Make sure you're not seen. Jan and Willem will go inside the building."

"What about the security guards?" Willem asked.

"You and Jan have to take care of them," Bauke answered. "They usually sit in the front office. Jan is an expert in taking out windows. Make sure you wear your masks and put socks over your shoes. I'll give you enough rope to tie up the guards. Use your weapons only as a last resort. Jan knows where they keep the food coupons, and he will fill several bags." Bauke looked at Jan. The younger man nodded. "Minne will be posted outside. Willem and Minne will take the bags from Jan. Then they'll bring them to the old shack behind the building. At seven-twenty my father and Klaas will pick up the bags. They'll have to hide them under their clothing and will leave the shack separately, ten minutes apart. Everybody got that so far?"

Johannes' spirits sank. Where did he come in? He chewed on his bottom lip and shifted his feet under the table.

"Father and Klaas will get the address of where to deliver the loot from Willem," Bauke continued. "I'll tell him as soon as I have confirmed my contact place. Johannes, your job is to warn Willem if anybody enters the building or if there are Germans in the area. You tap on the window at the rear of the building. Your hiding place is behind the shrubs at the side of the office. You'll have a good view of the main road and the bridge. You and Sietske will bicycle to the farm beside the drawbridge. Sietske will stay at the farm. You'll leave your bike there. You'll walk unnoticed to the building. At seven-thirty, you'll return to the farm. Then, you and Sietske will pedal home."

"And if things go wrong?" Johannes asked.

"You disappear unnoticed," Bauke answered.

Johannes looked over at Sietske. She smiled at him warmly. He wasn't sure what to think. Did he have the least risky job?

"Johannes can wear his normal clothes. Everybody else bring your mask and a revolver. Okay? Are there any questions?"

"Yes," Willem said as he stood up. "How can we be sure that the son of a collaborator is not going to leak our little plan?"

Johannes felt as if the man had slapped him in the face. How did Willem know? He had never seen the man before. Bauke must have informed him. So this was the test? To see if he could be trusted?

He pulled himself together, rose, looked Willem straight in the eye and said, "You just have to trust me."

"What guarantees do we have that you won't betray us?" Willem's dark eyes bored into him.

"There are no guarantees. This is war," Johannes answered. "I'll be here tomorrow night at six-fifteen."

Sietske walked Johannes to the door. In the hallway he turned around. "Don't come out with me tonight."

She clutched his sleeve. "Johannes, don't be angry. Can't you understand? These people are risking their lives. They don't know you."

"I do understand, but I am angry. Who told him about my father? I hate Willem. Who does he think he is? Good night. I'll see you tomorrow."

He opened the door and walked into the ice-cold night.

VIII

Identity – Family Secrets

SURVIVOR STATEMENTS

ALEX BUCKMAN
MARIETTE ROZEN DODUCK

Both Alex and Mariette were orphaned. Alex's parents were deported to Auschwitz Concentration Camp.

Mariette's hiding began at five, when the Germans invaded Belgium. When she was seven, the house where the family was hiding was raided by the SS. She saw her cousin's baby thrown out of the window, and witnessed her parents and brother arrested by the SS. Mariette never saw her family again.

Mariette: I hid my Jewish identity by living with non-Jewish families. A Mother Superior saved me once by hiding me in a rat-infested sewer. Later I was caught but released, when a decent German officer, who had been a friend of my brother's, pretended that I was his little sister.

Alex: I was a baby when the Germans invaded Brussels. I was placed first with a family and then in a Catholic orphanage.

When my aunt and uncle were released from the camp where they had been imprisoned for two years, they brought me home with them and I believed I was their son. I did not find out that they were not my parents until I was middle-aged.

LETTER FROM VIENNA

by Claudia Cornwall

A writer discovers her family's secret through a letter. She sets out to explore her Jewish roots. In the long and arduous process, her life and sense of identity undergo a profound change.

The Christmas Card

A woman with thick white hair and gray-green eyes is sitting at a white desk in a white room holding a white phone. Her skin is pale, the translucent ivory of a former redhead. This is my mother. I am at the other end of the line, a dark curly-haired woman with the same gray-green eyes. I am sitting on a blond cane chair in front of a bookshelf, holding a red phone. It is January 1989.

"Did you know?" I ask. I expect her to say that she did not.

"Yes," she answers instead.

"Why didn't you tell me?"

"If I have to choose between my loyalty to Daddy and my loyalty to you, Daddy comes first," my mother explains. "He never wants to talk about it. But now the Pandora's box is open."

I am calling because of a Christmas card I received the day before from my Uncle Günther in Vienna. On the front was a photograph taken in the Tyrolese Alps showing a church and snow and sunshine. When I opened the card, I found another photograph inside. This one was of my father at about the age of four. He was standing in a garden between two women, holding their hands. He gazed straight at the camera with a solemn expression.

I took the picture out of the card and laid it down, thinking I would frame it and hang it on my bedroom wall. Then I began to read my uncle's message. Writing in English, he opened with warm wishes and news about his family. There was nothing in his friendly tone or his remarks to prepare me for one sentence in the middle of his note. He offered it without explanation or comment. Then he went on to express the hope that our two families would meet in Austria for a holiday soon. He told me that a pacemaker implanted in my aunt's heart made her feel much better and sent us all his love and many kisses.

I stared back at the photograph. Again I saw three people in a garden nearly eighty years ago. One of the women was crouching. She wore a dark dress and a starched apron. On her lap were three picture books. The other woman stood. Around her shoulders was a printed shawl. Her dress was dark too, but the apron covering it was not so crisp. She smiled. I noticed the sunflowers, already tall but without their heads. The time was probably midsummer. As my father was born in July, perhaps the occasion was his birthday and the books I saw were presents.

I returned to the note. My uncle's riveting sentence was only twelve words long. He had written, "The lady standing up was our mother, who died in concentration camp." I had never heard about this. Ever.

I decided not to hang the photograph of my father and his mother on my bedroom wall. It made me uneasy. How would I speak about it to visitors? Should I say, "Yes, that's my grandmother and my father. In Austria, many years ago – on a summer vacation." Or, "My grandmother, you know; she died in a concentration camp." I put the picture back inside my uncle's Christmas card and returned the card to its envelope. Later I would place the envelope in a metal filing cabinet, but first it would sit by the phone for a couple of weeks.

Now, while talking to my mother about my uncle's note, I reach for it. Pulling out the photograph, I look at my grandmother's face. I notice her dark humorous eyes under their arched eyebrows. "Was she Jewish?" I ask.

"Yes," my mother replies.

"Was that why Daddy and Günther left Vienna?"

"Yes," she says again.

I have always felt that my father did not want to talk to me about his parents. My mother has told me most of what I know about them. I am beginning to understand why I felt so uncomfortable raising the subject with him.

I know that my grandmother was born in Poland, that her first name was Regine and that she was a good cook. My father still speaks of the blueberry *Buchteln* (small buns) she used to make. But beyond that is a blank. Now I feel as though she had died twice – first, somewhere in Eastern Europe, and secondly, in our heads, by not being remembered. I certainly had no idea she was Jewish. My father never observed any Jewish traditions or customs. I was baptized an Anglican and brought up in a vaguely Christian way. We always had a Christmas tree and presents but never went to church.

"What about my grandfather? Was he Jewish too?" I ask.

"Not completely, I think," my mother says. This stuns me again: there were Jewish relatives on both sides of my father's family.

My mother's answers to my questions are short and direct. Normally our conversations are much more discursive. I can ask her whether I should give my father a bird feeder as a present and within seconds find that we are talking about rats or the economy. But today there are no digressions and I miss them. I find myself wanting associations – a context – to help me make sense of what is happening. For once my mother provides none.

There is a part of my father I know nothing about. I wonder if he went to a synagogue as a young man. Did he have a bar mitzvah? When did he begin to celebrate Christmas? Was it strange to do so?

"Did my grandfather die in a camp too?" I want to know.

"I think he died before the war," my mother says. I feel relieved.

On a slushy Saturday afternoon a few days later, I visit my parents, Lore and Walter Wiener. Although I debate whether to phone ahead or not, in the end I just go. We live about half an hour apart by car. As I drive across the two bridges and through the downtown streets that separate us, I realize I am nervous. I do everything slowly and deliberately. I make certain all my car doors are locked when I park. Going down my parents' front walk, I look back at the water pooling in the footprints I leave in the wet snow.

My father opens the door for me. He is over eighty and slightly stooped. His eyes are blue and his hair, once dark blond, is now white. He smiles. "Where are the kids?" "With Gordon," I say. Still standing in the front hall, still wearing my coat, I bring out the photograph. "Your brother sent it to me." Then I hug my father. I feel his shoulder blades through his morning gown. He must have just had his afternoon nap, I think. "He told me what happened to your mother. I am so sorry." He takes the photograph, examines it closely, looks back at me and says, "Oh, you mean the Holocaust."

We sit down in the living room and my mother joins us. "Perhaps I should have warned him," she says to me. But, to my surprise, my father does not seem distressed about what I have discovered. For the first time that I can remember, he speaks to me at length about his family. He tells me about his paternal grandfather, Adalbert Wiener, who lived on a large farm and had seven children. My father's father, Rudolf, was the oldest. "I don't know what happened to these people," my father says.

We drink tea. The sky grows dark. Then my father talks about his mother's sister, Susanne. "She was married to Max Bergmann, a furniture dealer who sold goods on credit. One day, some of his customers came into the building and threw him down an elevator shaft. He survived, but after that, the whole Bergmann family committed suicide. They turned on the gas in their place." Max and Susanne, their son Alfred, their daughter Lotte, and a grandson about five or six years old all died.

"When did it happen?" I ask.

"The Germans came in the middle of March 1938. It was shortly after that."

"My mother's brother, Max Moldau," my father continues, "managed to get to England with the help of the Freemasons. My mother had hoped to be able to go to relatives in England too, but it didn't work out."

It is night now and cold. I have one more question to ask before I go. "Were your parents practising Jews?"

"My mother was."

"And your father?"

My father shrugs. "He went to the synagogue perhaps once a year for something like Yom Kippur."

I drive home along Vancouver's wet streets. The storm sewers are plugged with half-melted snow, and near the curbs the puddles are deep. Water smacks against the doors of my car. I am thinking about that spring, over half a century ago, when it started, when Austria became part of the Reich. Were the early flowers blooming along the Danube River? Were the leaves on the trees small and bright green? Was my father able to take any pleasure in such things?

Love Is So Far Away

I am alone in the house. My children are with a baby-sitter, my husband at work. I do not feel like phoning anyone. "Dearest Grandmother," I type. "Your sons are now old men. You would probably find it hard to believe that your dear Walter, my father, will celebrate his eighty-fifth birthday in four days. I have two children myself and I am always astonished at how quickly they grow.

"My father is in reasonably good health, although he complains about being tired. You were worried about whether he was eating well, but I think you can rest your mind on that score. My mother is an excellent cook. She has even learned to adapt her recipes to the fact that my father has mild diabetes and should not eat sugar. For his birthday, she will bake him a special chocolate cake using artificial sugar.

"I think you would be pleased to know that you have three grandchildren and five great-grandchildren! My two are a boy, Thomas, nearly six, and a girl, Natalia (we usually call her Talia), who is almost four. People say that Thomas looks much like my father. He is blond and has blue eyes. In fact, it was this family resemblance that prompted me to write to Uncle Günther. I wondered whether he had any pictures of my father as a young boy. We didn't have any, you see, in our photo albums. My uncle sent me a photograph. There were three people in it – my father, Anna Döld, your maid, and you. In a note, Uncle Günther wrote me that you had died in a concentration camp. I had never been told this.

"As you can imagine, it was a great shock. But I am glad that I know. It helps me to understand my father better. I am grateful, too, that I found out while he is still alive, so that we can talk about it.

"I have read two letters you sent to my father in Shanghai. I can see from them how much you loved both of your sons. In February 1937, my father wrote a poem. In it are the lines, 'All round is darkness, death and the grave/ Oh, love is so far away.' So it may have seemed to you too in your last days in Vienna and then in Eastern Europe, where you died. But I hope it would comfort you to know how well your love has endured.

Your dearest Walter was a kind and loving father and I, in turn, love my children dearly. They make me happy. When they are older I will talk to them about you and the legacy of love. With heartfelt greetings, Your granddaughter, Claudia."

I am not sure why I write this letter. In a sense it is useless, because it cannot change how my grandmother died and how she suffered. The words float. My grandmother will never receive them. And although I know all this the tears stop.

GOODBYE
MARIANNE

by Irene Kirstein Watts

*A one-act play about two weeks in
the life of a young Jewish girl living
in Berlin, Germany in 1938.
Friendless, expelled from school
by government decree, existence
becomes more difficult day by
day. Worst of all is her father's
disappearance and the secrecy that
surrounds it.*

Scene Five

MOTHER: I'm sorry I wasn't home, I just heard
              the announcement on the radio about
              Jewish students being expelled. I hurried
              to meet you. Was it very bad for you?

MARIANNE: No. Not too bad. At least I missed the test.
              Here are my records.

(MOTHER reads the teacher's comments.)

MOTHER: Look, that was really brave of Miss Stein
              to put "A diligent pupil." She could
              get into trouble for saying something
              complimentary like that. Don't worry
              too much. We'll work something out.

I'm sure the synagogue will set up classes.

MARIANNE: Great, we'll have broken windows all the time.

MOTHER: Marianne! I know it's difficult. We'll do the best we can.

MARIANNE: I know. I said it's all right. I understand.

MOTHER: How did you lose your key?

MARIANNE: I don't want to talk about it.

MOTHER: How can I help you if you won't tell me anything?

MARIANNE: It's the same for me – you never tell me anything – it's like I'm a baby or something.

MOTHER: I've never lied to you, you know that.

MARIANNE: Is Dad really away on business?

(Silence.)

He's in prison, isn't he? In one of those concentration camps, like the one Ruth's dad went to.

MOTHER: Not anymore.

MARIANNE: You see, you did lie to me. How do I know
                 you're not lying now? All these secrets,
                 and whispering, and people phoning and
                 not leaving messages. I have to know. Tell
                 me where he is.

MOTHER: I can't.

MARIANNE: Why not? Don't you trust me?

MOTHER: Of course I do, but suppose you were to
                 mention something, just accidentally, and
                 someone overheard you and reported us
                 to the Gestapo?

MARIANNE: Mother, I don't have anyone to play with
                 anymore, or to tell stuff to.

MOTHER: What about that boy? Marianne, no Jew is
                 safe at this time anywhere in Germany.
                 The government wants the people to hate
                 us. We are no longer considered citizens.

MARIANNE: Ernst's just a boy here on holidays from
                 the country. I wouldn't tell him anything.
                 We were talking about a book.

MOTHER: All right. You want the truth. It's so hard to talk about it. The police rounded up over a thousand men, your dad was one of them. They took him to Sachsenhausen Concentration Camp, and they took away all their clothes, and made them stand naked in the prison yard for twenty-four hours.

MARIANNE: *(Whispers.)* Oh, Daddy.

MOTHER: They hosed them down with ice water and beat them. Some died.

(MARIANNE holds her hands over her ears to shut out the words. Her MOTHER puts her arms around her.)

Now you know why I didn't tell you. But they let Daddy go. His employer spoke up for him, said he was a good worker, and he needed him. There are still some good people in Berlin.

MARIANNE: Where is he? Why isn't he here? I want to see him.

MOTHER: The store owner had to give his job to someone else. It's bad for business these days to employ a Jew. But at least he's not in jail. He's had to go underground. Into hiding. He's in a safe place. You mustn't worry.

MARIANNE: So that's where you go all the time.

MOTHER: Yes. I take a different route each time, and go to see him at different times of day, just in case I'm being watched. I take the bus, in the opposite direction sometimes, or go on the subway. Often I walk. He's fine – worried about us, of course. He sends you his love.

MARIANNE: Let me go with you next time please.

(The phone rings. MOTHER hurries to answer.)

MOTHER: Hello, Esther Kohn here. Yes, I can talk. Are you sure? Right away. Thank you for telling me. It's very kind of you. Goodbye. *(She hangs up. She is putting on her coat and hat as she speaks.)* I've got to go out again – I may be very late. Eat whatever you want. Lock the door after me.

MARIANNE: Has something happened to Daddy?

MOTHER: No, truly, and I promise I'll tell you every-thing when I get back.

(Exit. MARIANNE locks the door. Turns on the radio, and prepares to listen.)

ANNOUNCER: We interrupt this program of music by Richard Wagner to bring you highlights of the Führer's address to the nation.

(Sound of crowd cheering "Sieg Heil" three times. Soundtrack of Adolf Hitler's voice: "Ein Volk, Ein Land, Ein Führer." MARIANNE does some saluting, goose-stepping. She lowers the volume. Continuation of Wagner music, soft.)

MARIANNE: One people, one country, one Führer. It's a good thing there's only one of him. . . . *(Paces.)* How can it be one people? We're the people too, and they don't want us.

(There is a soft tap on the door. MARIANNE goes over to listen. Two more taps.)

Mother, is that you?

FATHER: Marianne, quickly, let me in.

(She unlocks the door. A figure in a long dark overcoat, wide soft-brimmed hat and muffler enters, shuts the door and hugs MARIANNE tightly. He muffles her scream.)

Don't call out, darling – we must be very quiet. Where's Mummy?

MARIANNE: I don't know, but she'll be back soon. Oh, Daddy, I knew you'd come back. Is it really you? You look like a gangster in a movie. Take off your things. I'll make you some coffee, in your favorite mug.

FATHER: I can't stay, darling. I'm sorry. It would put you both in too much danger, and my friends too. Please give Mummy a message. You must remember it. I don't want you to write it down. Just tell her I'm being moved tonight. When it's safe, someone will contact her with the new address.

MARIANNE: I won't forget. Why do the Nazis want you specially?

FATHER: Your old dad's a popular man, I suppose. Handsome, charming, debonair.

MARIANNE: Father, *tell* me.

FATHER: All right. I did a foolish thing. I sold a copy of a book written by a Jewish author. The customer reported me. Now I'm on the wanted list as a dangerous Jew. I have to stay underground, out of sight.

MARIANNE: Just for selling a book!

FATHER: There's a craziness in this country at the moment. Let's hope it won't last long.

MARIANNE: Do you think we'll ever be together again like a family?

FATHER: We can be together in our thoughts, even if we don't live in the same house. Not even Hitler can stop us loving each other. I *must* go. Lock up after me, Marianne. Remember the message. I love you both.

MARIANNE: Me too. Goodbye. Be careful, Daddy.

(FATHER opens the front door. Pauses to check the hall, hurries away. MARIANNE locks up. Exhausted with emotion, she curls up on the sofa and falls asleep. Musical interlude.)

ON SAINT
KATERINE'S DAY

by Lili Berger

> *During the Holocaust, Jewish
> parents were desperate to hide
> their children from the Nazis,
> hoping one day to reclaim them.
> If the parents died, children grew
> up in ignorance of their true
> parentage, or discovered their
> roots years later by accident.*

From **Found Treasures: Stories by Yiddish Women Writers**
Translated by Frieda Forman and Ethel Raicus

Katerine Vrublevska had thick black curly hair, large, dark velvet eyes, a pale, dreamy, longish face and was fifteen years old.

Her classmates described her skin color as "café au lait." She knew she was a beauty, how could she not know since they always told her so. Among her school-friends she looked like an exotic rose by some chance growing amidst wild flowers. Ever since she could remember she had been called "black beauty," and when her Uncle Karol, a pharmacist from Warsaw, came to visit, he brought gifts for the "pretty gypsy." Uncle Karol loved her dearly, her aunt did too, but now their love seemed so strange to Katerine, so distant, even her mother's love. Why did she hide it from her? Everyone knew, but she didn't. That's why Fat Theresa felt free to make fun of her.

Probably everyone, everyone was laughing at her; she had understood nothing, now she understood very well, now she remembered everything. Sundays, at church, she would feel them looking at her strangely. "Because you are a beauty," her mother would tell her. Not true, it was because of something else, all of them, all of them were always looking at her; she had never guessed, was never suspicious. Now she knew, this morning she finally understood everything, now she remembered how they would sometimes say to her, "You're different, somehow." Why hadn't she caught on? She probably wouldn't have caught on, even now, if it weren't for Fat Theresa, that red-faced girl always blurted out what others wouldn't say, she'd often dropped hints.

What did Theresa have against her? She never did her any harm – on the contrary, while others ridiculed her, disliked her, imitated her duck's waddle, Katerine wouldn't. That one was so silly and fat as a barrel, her face puffy, red as a beet; learning was hard for her, she couldn't absorb it. But was it Theresa's fault? Wouldn't she have wanted to be pretty and clever? Katerine had always sympathized with her, had never done her any wrong, and still Theresa never had a good word for her, only barbs, insinuations, always resentment, until finally Theresa had blurted out, "You shouldn't bring flowers to Sister Katerine! It's not your place! It has nothing to do with you!"

"Why not with me?"

"Because . . . because . . . you're a Jew!"

"You're one yourself!" Katerine answered impulsively and immediately regretted it. Everyone laughed and Fat Theresa with the red face laughed the loudest of all, gasping with laughter, jeering.

"Who's a Jew? Me or her?" the fat girl asked triumphantly and again burst out with mocking laughter.

That laughter had cut and stung Katerine like a whip. She fled, escaping their laughter, found her way to the convent which wasn't far from the forest. She didn't feel the cold wind on her face, walked quickly, almost running, as though pursued by their laughter. The flowers' wrapping came apart, she paid no attention. Every year she brought flowers to Sister on her saint's day, it had always been a pleasure for her. Now she arrived at the convent out of breath, distraught, and nervously rang the bell. When Sister Katerine appeared at the door, she fell into her arms weeping.

"My child, what happened to you? You're crying on such a day? On the day of our patron saint? Tell me, what happened to you?"

"They . . . they . . . said that it's not my saint's day, Saint Katerine's Day, that . . . it doesn't belong to me, that . . . that I'm a Jew."

"Don't listen to such foolish talk, my child. People like to smear others, they don't have God in their hearts, they fill their time with evil talk. . . ."

"Why do they think I'm a . . . ? Why? I ask you, tell me, I want to know why, I want to know what I am." Katerine pleaded tearfully.

"What are you? You're a good Christian, a Christian for a long time now, since 1942. You were probably a year old, certainly not two; foolishness . . . not worth talking about, people love to babble –" the nun held herself back, sorry that she'd said this much.

"Once . . . was I a Jew once?" Katerine persisted with a new question and her eyes, full of tears, begged for an answer.

"You're a good Christian like your mother. Go, my child, go home, I'm busy now, it's our name day. Remember, today you mustn't cry; on Saint Katerine's Day, one doesn't cry; a great day, she was a great saint. Thank you for the flowers, you always remember, you're a good Christian . . . go home, my child. . . ."

The way home from the convent could be shortened by going through a small field, then across a little bridge over the stream. Katerine didn't like that path; this time she took the back road, walking quickly, gasping for air, overwhelmed. Only at home did she calm down a bit, began to make sense of Sister's vague words, counting the years, remembering various insinuations, overheard conversations about Jewish children protected in convents. She did know something about these things but never gave it much thought, had read several books about how those people perished. Her mother wouldn't let her read such books; "You'll get sick, you mustn't read that." Now she understood why her mother had taken *Maria's Farewell* from her hands, why her mother always avoided questions, didn't answer, squirming exactly the way Sister Katerine had. She wouldn't put up with it any longer; she would have to find everything out, figure it all out herself, and she'd force her mother, her mother would have to tell her the truth, she'd beg with tears, she would have to know today, today her mother would have to. . . .

"I thought you were lying down, but here you are sitting staring; you said you had a headache, so why are you fretting?"

Her mother's voice interrupted Katerine's thoughts. She let her finish, raised her head, and looked at her mother suspiciously, the way you look at a stranger whose closed face you want to decipher, but she was immediately ashamed of herself and lowered her head.

"What's wrong, daughter? I can tell that something's happened; tell your mother; you've always told me everything. You trust your mother after all; tell the truth; you've never held back from me."

"And you, mother, have never withheld anything from me? Told the truth?"

"I think . . . why should I hide, when you ask, if it's appropriate, I tell you . . . but what kind of talk is this, my daughter? You're not speaking nicely to your mother," said Magdalena tenderly and with wily humor.

"I want to know . . . I want to know . . . who I am; they said that . . . that I'm a Jew, everyone, everyone knows it, they look at me. . . ."

Magdalena Vrublevska turned pale, held on to the bed railing with both hands. It was suddenly difficult for her to remain standing. Slowly she sat down beside her daughter, sat mute as though the power of speech had been taken from her, and then she quietly answered, "You accept all this gossip and take it seriously, fuss over every foolishness. . . ."

"I want to know who I am," Katerine interrupted her. "I want to know the truth!" By now she was shouting.

"Who drummed such thoughts into your head?" Her mother tried raising her voice.

"Everyone, everyone knows; Sister Katerine also told me a while ago that I'm . . . no, Sister also didn't want to tell me

everything, didn't want to answer . . . put me off with –"
Katerine burst into tears, holding her face in both hands and
sobbing. Magdalena moved closer to her, holding her, pressing
her against herself, trying to convince her in a soft, shaking
voice, "Who are you? You're my daughter, my whole life. I love
you as you love me, your mother. Why pay attention to . . . ?
Why? Why listen to foolish prattle?"

"I want to know . . . I must know. Tell me the truth! Tell
me!"

"Fine, I will . . . tomorrow. First, calm down, my foolish
child. Come and eat, my little fool."

"To you I'm still a little child, a 'little fool.' I want you to
tell me everything right now!" And Katerine burst into even
more violent weeping.

"So, good, let it be, but stop crying. That's why I didn't
want to tell you in the first place. You make a fuss about any
little trifle. I beg you, daughter, there's nothing to cry about.
Promise me, my child, that you won't exaggerate things.
You're a grown girl now, and crying is unbecoming. Is life so
bad for us?"

Magdalena caught her breath, silent for a while, thinking of
how to go on with this painful conversation with her daughter.

"If you want, I'll tell everything. But it mustn't change
anything between us. What can it possibly mean to us? Isn't
that so? Do you promise me, daughter dear?"

Katerine nodded and blurted through her tears, "I promise,
but tell me everything; tell me the whole truth."

Mother and daughter sat clinging to one another. Katerine,
sobbing quietly from time to time, dried her eyes. Magdalena
Vrublevska was silent for some time. What she had feared of

late had come to pass. Katerine was an intelligent girl, but so sensitive; she felt everything so intensely. Now she could no longer pull the wool over her eyes. She must tell her the truth, but how? She had thought about it many times; in her imagination, that daybreak reappeared. She covered her eyes with her hands, steeled herself, and began, "I adopted you, Sister Katerine probably told you that. You were tiny, really tiny; you were with Sister Katerine. I adopted you and from that time on you've been my daughter and I your mother."

"From the beginning, start at the beginning. Where did Sister Katerine get me? Tell me, tell me from the beginning, everything, everything, I beg of you."

Magdalena remained silent, her face clouded over. She clasped her daughter more tightly to herself, stroking her hair, and then began again.

"It was in 1942, dawn, still dark. They were being driven on this road, the back road that leads to the forest; they passed close to our house. I lay in bed shaking as if I had a fever. The wailing and howling was unbearable, wailing and howling, then an echo of gunshot, then – silence. There was no question of sleep after that; my heart was heavy, in my ears the wailing rang but outside it was as silent as the graveyard. Suddenly, I heard whimpering, like a sick kitten, then something like the choked cry of a baby. I got out of bed to listen at the door. Everything was quiet; I stood there a few minutes and went back to bed.

"It was daylight at last but the town was lifeless; people were still afraid to go out. It was a Sunday; no-one went to work, they stayed indoors. It was very stuffy and I wanted some air, so I carefully opened the front shutter and stuck my head out and . . . a parcel at the door, some sort of strange parcel, a kind of bundle. I panicked; we were afraid of everything. I closed the window but, recalling the whimpering earlier on, I opened the door a crack. The bundle stirred. I looked around to see whether anyone was watching, pulled the bundle in and untied it . . . a child . . . seemingly smothered; the sop had fallen out of the little mouth. I put my ear to the child; it was breathing. I took it out of the knotted little quilt; it looked frail. It occurred to me to pour warm, sweet water into the little mouth; it wasn't long before it began to cry, first quite softly, then louder and louder. Oh my God, a catastrophe! Then I really panicked; such a risk, everyone knew I was a widow, alone; my child had died three years earlier, and here a child, and one so dark, my God. I quickly stopped your mouth with the sop; packed it with wet sugar. I was so terrified that it would cry; I was almost out of my mind with fright, what to do with the child? It was then that I remembered Sister Katerine, she was so compassionate and wise; gave good advice; she wouldn't refuse. I dressed quickly, put the child into the vegetable basket, packing the sop with wet sugar, covered the basket with an old towel, put the flowers from the vase on top, as well as some vegetables I had prepared to take to the convent on Sunday. Fortunately you didn't cry, you were hungry and sucked on the sugar. When Sister Katerine removed your clothing to bathe you a note fell out of your little right sock: 'Merciful people, save this child; God will reward you.' Then the name. Date of birth wasn't given, probably forgotten. Sister Katerine fed you, then made out a certificate of baptism. It was Saint Katerine's Day, just like today; you were given her name and I was forbidden to come to see you, just as well. After that, difficult times befell me."

Magdalena Vrublevska stopped as though the telling had exhausted her and looking at Katerine saw her strange expression: the girl was staring straight ahead, mouth open, not a muscle in her face moving, as though everything had frozen from shock. Magdalena waited for her to respond, then could wait no longer. "My child, should I go on to the end?" Katerine only nodded and two full, round tears rolled down from her dark eyes. Magdalena, now hurrying to finish, spoke in chaotic, unfinished sentences.

"Told myself that if I survived, you'd be my child; my little girl died, God sent an unfortunate child, had to wait. After the war my situation was difficult, had to come back to myself; thanks to Uncle Karol, he helped me a lot, always loved you; according to the baptismal certificate, you were four years old. Sister Katerine led me to a dark little girl and, pointing to me, said to her, 'This is your mother, a good mother, you must love her. . . .' Since then, I have been so happy; grew to love you like my own child, what's the difference? You really are my own child, my only daughter. I was so. . . ."

The words stuck in her throat, choking. Both were silent now, their heartbeats could be heard in the stillness. Magdalena became alarmed at Katerine's silence and said, "You see, my child, I've told everything, hidden nothing; you know every-thing now."

"Not everything yet."

"What more do you want to know?"

"What was my name?"

"Miriam. Miriam Zack."

"And my parents?"

"Sister Katerine may know."

"The note, my note? I want to see. . . ."

"I'll ask Sister, perhaps she has it, perhaps. . . . But be patient, better I go myself, it's more fitting."

"And family? Relatives? Do I have someone . . . ?"

"How can we know that? You have . . . me, Uncle Karol, Auntie, aren't we your family? Am I not a mother to you and you a daughter to me?"

"Yes, yes, you are, of course you are, but –" and Katerine broke into tears again.

Shortly after Saint Katerine's Day, mother and daughter together composed and mailed the following notice to the Red Cross, Missing Relatives Division: "Miriam Zack, daughter of Leyzer and Rivke Zack from the city of T., seeks relatives, wherever they may be, within the country or abroad. Reply."

SHHH

by Deborah Schnitzer

He shoulders her
Eyes wrapped in a blanket she has given up crying

noises kill people
"Shhh."

If she should say the name of her brother who was bent by
the road
She will shatter the glasses her father is wearing
When her mother screams

"Shhh."
This is the sound of today and tomorrow
This is everyone's new name
Dipped in darkness

IX

"The Holocaust and After"

SURVIVOR STATEMENT

CELINA KOLIN LIEBERMAN

I was born in Zbaraz, Ukraine, and was ten years old when the Germans invaded Lvov, Poland in 1941. A wonderful Catholic Polish woman hid me. I learned to do farmwork, speak like the villagers, and pretend I could not read or write. I was fourteen years old at the end of the war. My relatives had perished and I believed I was the only surviving Jew on Earth. In the Displaced Persons Camp, I was asked if I wanted to go to Canada. I was without a family or a country, and said yes.

On the boat I always took a piece of bread from dinner. All the children hid bread under their pillows. We landed at Halifax in February 1948. I was one of 1,123 Jewish War Orphans to be admitted from Europe.

SURVIVOR STATEMENT

RITA SMILOVICI AKSELROD

I was born in Romania. I was not allowed to continue in public school, and was made to wear the yellow star. When Romanian soldiers plundered Jewish homes, sometimes killing the residents, we hid from them in a shack in the yard. My brother was sent to a labor camp.

After the war, I lived in a Displaced Persons Camp. I arrived in Vancouver in 1951.

THE HOLOCAUST
AND AFTER

by Mordecai Richler

From **Shovelling Trouble**

Speaking for myself, I am a believer in obligatory voyages, Gehenna being as necessary as the heavenly spheres, and so I've been to Germany as well as Jerusalem.

On my first day in Munich, in 1955, I went to meet a friend at the American Army Service Club, formerly Hitler's *Haus der Kunst*. Drifting into the lobby, I was confronted by a life-size cardboard hillbilly which held a poster announcing that Friday would be "Grand Ole Op'ry Night." Over the information desk, there was another announcement that I used in my novel, *St. Urbain's Horseman*. This one set out Saturday's diversions. Visiting GIs were assured that promptly at 1400 hours a bus would leave for nearby Dachau: "BRING YOUR CAMERAS! VISIT THE CASTLE AND THE CREMATORIUM."

I was in Germany again in 1963, this time to write a piece about the Royal Canadian Air Force base on the out-skirts of Baden-Baden. Young, distinctly small-town Canadian schoolteachers attached to the air base breathlessly assured me the Germans were "a simply fantastic people." So modern, so clean, "We have a lot to learn from them," a science teacher told me. "From their leisurely way of life."

The next evening I went to the Social Center, mixing with teenagers at a dance. "What have you seen in Europe?" I asked them.

"Venice."

"A bullfight in Barcelona."

"Dachau."

Dachau. The boy was only fourteen. His parents, he said, had taken him to Dachau when he was twelve. To my astonishment, most of the other children had been there too.

"Do you know what Dachau is?" I asked. "They used to punish people there."

"Naw. Like it was extermination."

"No, no. They just hung guys there. They never used the gas chambers."

"Who told you that?" I asked.

"The Germans."

I asked if they had found Dachau a chilling place.

"It's not used any more, but."

"Yeah, it was only during the war. They used to torture guys there."

"Why?"

"Um, there were too many prisoners so they had to kill some off."

"Jews were against Hitler so they had to exterminate them."

"What else?" I asked.

"It was," a boy said, "an unusual place to visit."

ALIEN

by Kenneth Sherman

My student (aged 21)
has never heard of Auschwitz
His eyes are vacuous
like one of those aliens on *Star Trek*.

He's seen every single show,
can tell me Spock's first name,
the thousand and one ways
Capt. Kirk faced death.

Yet he has never heard
the names Goebbels, Rudolf Hess –
and Hitler now
some hard luck hero.

On his arm a tattooed knife
has got it in for a heart.
He dreams beer river
and the ultimate overhead drive.

Perhaps minds like his
are controlled from some
far away hostile planet.

Bleep, bleep. Bleep, bleep.

Someone
something
speaking through him
of a future dark and brutal.

ASSIGNMENT: ANNE FRANK

by Ellen Schwartz

Mr. Andrews came into the classroom carrying a stack of paperbacks, which he piled on his desk. Then he took up his usual teaching position, perched on the edge of the desk, one long leg swinging.

"Good morning, people. We're going to start a new book today."

"Please, not like the last one," Jill muttered, and everybody laughed. She didn't care if Mr. Andrews got mad at her, *The Mill on the Floss* had been a total bore. She hoped the next book would be more interesting and fun.

Mr. Andrews smiled. "Not at all like the last one, Jill. Our next book is *The Diary of a Young Girl* by Anne Frank."

A murmur rippled through the class.

"Aw, Mr. Andrews, do we have to read that?" Rob Kinnear said. "It's so depressing."

"So scary, you mean," Zara Mahrani put in.

Mr. Andrews nodded. "True, it's not an easy read. But still a very important book. Do you realize that Anne Frank was just about your age when she wrote it?"

A chill shivered up Jill's back. She'd never read the diary – despite Grandma Ida's frequent urgings – had never wanted to. But of course she knew who Anne Frank was, and what had happened to her. You couldn't be Jewish and not know. But to think that Anne was her age when it had happened. Only fourteen, and hiding for your life . . . when every footstep could mean death. . . . With a shudder, Jill cut off her thoughts. It was too awful to think about.

She tuned back in. Someone must have asked about Anne Frank, because Mr. Andrews was explaining. ". . . a young Dutch Jewish girl who died in World War II. Actually, she was German – the family had moved to Amsterdam from Frankfurt several years earlier, after the Nazis came to power in Germany."

Jill shivered again. She didn't want to hear this.

"When the Nazis invaded Holland, the Frank family went into hiding in some secret rooms above Mr. Frank's factory," Mr. Andrews went on. "Anne was thirteen. They lived there for two years, until they were discovered and sent to concentration camps."

Jill tried not to listen, but Mr. Andrews's voice cut through the silence that had fallen in the room.

"Anne died only two months before the liberation of Holland. She was just shy of fifteen."

A sigh swept through the class.

"But Anne had been given a diary for her thirteenth birthday," Mr. Andrews continued. "In it she recorded her thoughts and her feelings. Her first love. Her arguments with her parents. Her frustration at being cooped up. Her secret hopes and dreams. Somehow the diary was left behind when the Franks were arrested, and after the war her father, the only member of the family to survive, found it and had it published.

"Now, as you're reading, I want you to be thinking about what Anne's story has to tell us today. What does it mean for us at the beginning of the twenty-first century? Sure, it's important as the story of one girl's life, and as a chronicle of the 1940s, but I want you to look at the bigger picture, too. See what issues it raises that are still relevant today. Any questions?"

"Yeah, when are the essays due and how long do they have to be?" Carlos Fuentes asked.

"As usual, Carlos, getting to the heart of the matter," Mr. Andrews said with a chuckle. He consulted a desk calendar. "One month from today. And let's say a thousand words." He considered. "No, make that fifteen-hundred. This is a big subject."

A groan arose from the class. Mr. Andrews started passing out books. "You can use the rest of the period to start reading."

Jill glanced at the cover, then shrank back as Anne Frank's eyes seemed to bore into hers. A shudder went through her. She put her hand over the cover, blocking out Anne's face. It was as if she wanted to block out the very idea of Anne Frank. Fiercely, desperately, she did not want to read the book. Didn't know why, didn't care, just didn't. *Couldn't.*

But against her will, Anne Frank's eyes drew her back. Jill withdrew her hand – and saw only the face of a girl, a girl about her age. Not a very pretty face at that, thin, pinched, with a protruding chin and a too-wide mouth in an irritating smile.

A homely girl in grainy black and white. Well, naturally it was grainy, the picture was old. 1940-ish. . . . She calculated mentally. Sixty years ago. Cripes, that was old. *Ancient.*

An idea flashed into her mind – and a way to get out of the assignment. She raised her hand. "Mr. Andrews?"

"Yes, Jill?"

"I don't think we should have to read this book."

"Really." A smile started curling at the corners of Mr. Andrews' mouth. "That's a most unusual statement. Would you mind explaining why?"

"'Cause it's old news. It's past and gone. I mean, it's horrible what happened, I'm not saying it isn't. But it's over. It's been over for nearly sixty years. Why dredge it up again?"

Jessica Steinman's hand shot up. "Jessica?" Mr. Andrews said.

"I can't believe you're saying that, Jill," Jessica said in an outraged tone. "There's still racism, still anti-Semitism. You're a Jew. You should know."

"I do know," Jill snapped. God, Jessica drove her crazy. She was like "Super-Jew" – wore a huge Star of David, constantly blabbed about her Jewish youth group and how she couldn't wait to make her *aliyah* in Israel. She *dripped* Jewishness.

"But it's not like back then," Jill argued. "The Nazis aren't trying to take over the world anymore. I mean, if that stuff was still going on, OK, I could see why we'd need to read it. But this is Canada. People get along –"

"Tell that to the French and English," someone said.

"OK, OK," Jill admitted, "but come on, it's still not like the Nazis slaughtering the Jews. I just don't think we need to get hit over the head with it anymore."

Mr. Andrews perched on the edge of his desk, smiling his teasing half-smile, clearly enjoying himself. "So the world doesn't need to learn the lesson of the Holocaust?"

"We've learned it," Jill said. "That's the point. What happened to Anne Frank could never happen again. People would never let it."

"What about Africa?" Winnie Kinchella said in her musical voice. "Where my family's from, in Uganda, one tribe slaughtered my people. Now we're killing them."

"It's horrible, I agree," Jill said, "but it's still not the same as putting millions of people into concentration camps and gassing them. And besides, that's there. This is here. I mean, look at our class. We've got all kinds of races and colors in here, and everybody gets along."

Good-natured grumbling arose.

"Except Kinnear. I can't stand you, Kinnear."

"I hate everybody."

"It's those damn Chinese, building all those monster houses," Jason Kwan said, and everyone laughed.

Jill laughed, too. "See, Mr. Andrews? That proves my point. We can laugh at ourselves. There's not that kind of deep hatred anymore. Times have changed."

"You can never change what happened, Jill!" Jessica Steinman said in an outraged tone.

"I don't mean that, Jessica, for crying out –"

"I had relatives wiped out in the Holocaust –"

"So did I!" Jill thought of Grandma Ida's family, who'd died at Auschwitz.

"– practically my entire family, sent to the gas ovens. We can't forget!"

"We're not forgetting," Jill insisted. "That's not what I'm saying. But let's move on, for goodness' sake. Why don't we read about something that's happening today instead?"

"Like what?" Mr. Andrews said.

Jill grasped for examples. "Like . . . oh, I don't know, like street kids, or the rain forest, or something?"

There was a buzz of voices. Mr. Andrews waited for the arguments to go back and forth, then held up his hand. "It's a very interesting point you raise, Jill," he said with his customary twinkle. "I think you're dead wrong, but you're entitled to your opinion. So I tell you what." He looked around the room. "I'll throw it open. 'Why We Need to Read *The Diary of a Young Girl* – or Why We Don't.' Give me an argument on one side or the other. In thesis essay form, of course."

He looked straight at Jill as he added, "I look forward to some very interesting papers."

Jill grinned back. Yes! This was going to be a cinch. She'd ace the paper – and get out of reading that stupid book.

I SAT IN LOEWS THEATRE STARING AT THE MOVIE SCREEN

by Jean Little

***From* Too Young to Fight,**
compiled by Priscilla Galloway

During the late forties and early fifties, my parents began employing a procession of "displaced people" whom the war had uprooted and set adrift. The Yamazakis came first. They were a Japanese couple, middle-aged with young adult children. They had been forcibly uprooted from their peaceful life in British Columbia and sent to a Canadian internment camp. When they were not allowed to return to the West Coast in spite of peace having been declared, they came to Guelph. One of their daughters was a student nurse at the hospital where Mother and Dad worked as doctors.

All through the war, my brothers and sister and I had not been allowed to speak of "Japs" as the other kids did. We were sternly reminded that we had many Japanese friends and that it was wrong to speak so of a people who were already suffering.

Mother and Dad also had friends who had perished in Japanese prisoner of war camps but what they endured was not relayed to us until we were grown. Now we were told firmly not to call people without homes DPs, as most people did, but New Canadians.

After the Yamazakis relocated, we met a Latvian family, a Dutch girl younger than I who had been sent away by her mother during the worst fighting in Holland, and a Russian couple. Inevitably, we also met many of their friends and relations. We heard about loneliness, fear, loss, shattered dreams as we did the dishes together or helped make beds. Although I was a self-absorbed teenager who wanted others to listen to my problems and resented having to share my parents' limited time with suffering humanity, I could not help being appalled and moved sometimes to tears by the pain and terror and loss through which these survivors had lived.

Among the people who came to Canada to wash dishes, scrub floors, cut grass, and shovel snow were lawyers, ministers, teachers, and professors. They had little or nothing left of their vanished lives. Always, wherever they went, the shadow of war followed them, diminishing their dreams, stealing their youth, invalidating their education. It was years before most of them felt they belonged in Canada. Some never did.

Then I was old enough to go away to college. During my second year, I picked up a new book called *The Diary of a Young Girl* by Anne Frank. Unaware of her capture, torture, and death, I read along, aching for her in her imprisonment, yet confidently waiting for the war to end and her freedom to be given back to her. When I turned the last page and found out that she never did escape, that all her worst fears came true in scenes of brutality and terror beyond my imagining, I fell apart and wept for hours. The following day, even though I attended classes and worked on essays again, I went about burdened with a horror I could not shake.

Mother had comforted me as a child by repeating, over and over, "Jean, it's only a story. Everything will be all right in the end."

But what had happened to Anne Frank was not just a story. It was a darkness with no stars. Everything went tragically wrong in the end. And this had been brought about by human beings like me. The Nazis who broke in on her hiding place had begun life as tiny babies, had taken their first steps, had been rocked to sleep like me. What had turned them into monsters who could use people so cruelly? What had twisted their humanity out of shape? Could I ever lose mine?

I did not know. I still do not fully understand. But I do know that the movies and books which finish up with the joyous homecoming of the gallant hero, limping only a little, lie. Real war wounds maim you for life. Fear haunts the dreams of children caught in war even when they become grandparents. Although I lived through the war years cocooned in my cozy Canadian childhood, the life stories told to me by people who had survived World War II, and a book written by a teenager who had not, taught me that war has no happy ending. Although I still live in a cocoon called Canada, I try not to forget.

HALL OF REMEMBRANCE

by Leo Vogel

Mr. and Mrs. Reimerink, who saved the writer's life during the war, were declared to be "Righteous People." After their deaths their names were inscribed on the walls of the Garden of Remembrance at Yad Vashem in Jerusalem.

I watch a wisp of smoke
ride from the perpetual flame,
that burns gently
in the Hall of Remembrance.
It twirls like a helix,
holding on to the secrets of life and death,
gathering the memories of parents;
mine and theirs,
and my other parents.

I float with it
before it disappears,
through a hole in the roof
into the cloudless sky over Jerusalem.
Trapped feelings trickle from me
as they escape my cavern of remembrance,
and mingle with this ghostly smoke.

I listen to the song of the Cantor,
rolling off the boulders of the wall,
where memories are steeped in pain.
Each note, explodes another tear in my head.
I fear that I too will die –
a feeling, strangely comforting.

I hear halting sobs around me
as we stand to commemorate the brave.
My sister, who's also not my sister,
stands in the place where her parents
ought to have been.
Her eyes turn inward,
reflecting on those bestial times,
long gone and still present.

TIME LINE

1933

- Hitler becomes the Chancellor of Germany.
- Dachau Concentration Camp is established.
- Public burnings of books by authors whom the Nazis disapproved of begins.

1935

- The Nuremberg Laws strip German Jews of their citizenship. A Jew is defined according to his/her grandparents.

1938

- Germany takes over Austria.
- Jewish passports are marked with a letter J.
- Night of the Broken Glass (*Kristallnacht*) is a two-day state-led attack on Jewish homes, businesses, offices, and synagogues. 30,000 male Jews, 16 years and over, are sent to concentration camps.
- Jewish students are expelled from German schools.
- The first *Kindertransport* for children at risk leaves Germany for Great Britain.

1939

- German troops occupy Czechoslovakia.
- Germany invades Poland.
- World War II begins.

- Jews in German-occupied countries are forced to wear the yellow star.

1940

- Germany occupies Denmark, Southern Norway, The Netherlands, Belgium, Luxembourg, and France.
- Auschwitz Concentration Camp is established.
- The Warsaw Ghetto is sealed.

1941

- Germany attacks Yugoslavia, Greece, and the Soviet Union.
- 34,000 Jews are massacred at Babi Yar, near Kiev.
- Auschwitz II (Birkenau) Concentration Camp is built in order to expedite the murder of Jews, Gypsies, and other ethnic groups.
- Adolf Eichmann becomes head of Jewish Affairs of Reich Security.
- Japan attacks the United States of America at Pearl Harbor.
- The United States of America declares war on Germany and Japan.

1942

- The Wannsee Conference in Berlin initiates the planned murder of European Jewry (The Final Solution).
- Mass deportations to Auschwitz begin.

1943

- The Warsaw Ghetto uprising erupts. Jewish fighters hold out against the Nazi war machine for almost four weeks before the Ghetto is razed.
- Denmark is the only country that succeeds in rescuing most of its Jewish population.

1944

- Nazis invade Hungary and deport close to 400,000 Jews to death camps.
- D-Day – the Allies invade Normandy, France.

1945

- Death marches from concentration camps to Germany.
- Liberation of Buchenwald – the first concentration camp in Germany to be liberated by the Allies.
- Death of Adolf Hitler.
- Fall of Germany to the Allies.
- End of the Third Reich.
- Bombing of Hiroshima.
- Bombing of Nagasaki.
- Surrender of Japan.
- World War II ends.

FURTHER READING

Titles marked with an * are suitable for ages 10+. Others are for mature readers 13+.

* Auerbach, Inge. *I am a Star: Child of the Holocaust – A Childhood in Terezin*. New York: Puffin Penguin, 1993. The author recreates life in the "model" concentration camp, where only one hundred children out of fifteen thousand who arrived there survived.

Dumbach, Annette and Newboard, Jud. *Shattering the German Night: The Story of the White Rose*. Boston: Little, Brown. 1986. The story of German students who formed an anti-Nazi organization against the régime, and were executed.

Elliach, Yaffa. *Hasidic Tales of the Holocaust*. New York: Random House, First Vantage Books, 1988. Stories told to the author by survivors. The tales have a mythic, folk quality and are set in the time of the Third Reich.

* Fox, Anne L. & Abraham-Podietz, Eva. *Ten Thousand Children*. Springfield, NJ: Behrmann House Inc., 1998. True stories by children who escaped the Holocaust on the *Kindertransport*.

* Frank, Anne. *The Diary of a Young Girl: The Definitive Edition*. Susan Massotty, trans. Otto H. Frank and Mirjam Pressler, eds. New York: Doubleday (Anchor Books), 1995. Secret journal entries by a young girl hidden in Amsterdam during the war.

Gilbert, Martin. *The Holocaust*. London: Collins, 1986. Also *The Atlas of the Holocaust*. Toronto: Lester Publishing, 1994. By the author of *The Boys: Triumph Over Adversity*. Vancouver: Douglas and McIntyre, 1996.

* Holm, Anne. *I am David*. Puffin Penguin, 1963. Translated from the Danish by Methuen, London, 1965. A boy escapes from a concentration camp and flees across Europe, seeking his family in Denmark.

* Joffo, Joseph. *A Bag of Marbles*. Boston: Houghton Mifflin, 1974. A true story about the adventures of two young boys fleeing the Nazis in occupied France

Koonitz, Claudia. *Mothers in the Fatherland: Women, the Family and Nazi Politics*. New York: St Martin's, 1987. An account of every aspect of female life in the Third Reich; how Catholic, Protestant, and Jewish women raised their families in a time of terror.

* Kerr, Jean. *The Day that Hitler Stole Pink Rabbit*. First published in Great Britain, 1971. William Collins Sons & Co. Ltd. The true story of Anna and her family's flight from the Nazis. An exciting and humorous account of one refugee family in 1933.

Leitner, Isabella and Leitner, Irving. *Isabella: From Auschwitz to Freedom*. New York: Anchor Books, 1994. The true story of the Katz sisters' internment, their eventual rescue by the Russians, and their emigration to New York.

Levi, Primo. *Survival in Auschwitz*. New York: Collier, 1961. The classic account by the great Italian writer.

Lifton, Betty Jane. *The King of Children, a Biography of Janusz Korczak*. New York: Farrar, Strauss and Giroux, 1988.

* Rogasky, Barbara. *Smoke and Ashes: The Story of the Holocaust.* New York: Holiday House, 1988. A comprehensive, lucid account, excellent for student readers. Contains many photographs and a selected glossary.

* Sachs, Marilyn. *A Pocket Full of Seeds.* New York: Puffin Penguin, 1994. Nicole must hide from the Nazis, when they capture her parents.

* Siegel, Aranka. *Upon the Head of a Goat: A Childhood in Hungary 1939–44.* New York: Penguin Puffin, 1994. A memoir of life in a small Hungarian town and the approaching menace of the Nazis. The sequel, *Grace in the Wilderness*, continues Aranka's story after the liberation of Auschwitz.

* Spiegelman, Art. *Maus: I and II. A Survivor's Tale.* Pantheon Books, a division of Random House, Inc. New York, and simultaneously in Canada by Random House of Canada Ltd., Toronto, 1973. The cartoonist's sophisticated view of Nazism and its aftermath.

* Steiner, Connie Colker. Illustrated by Denis Rodler. *Shoes for Amélie.* Montreal: Lobster Press, 2001. Lucien's parents hide a Jewish girl in the remote village of Le Chambon-sur-Lignon. The young narrator writes movingly of wartime France. Suitable for ages eight to twelve.

* Volávkova, Hana, editor, U.S. Holocaust Memorial Museum. *I Never Saw Another Butterfly.* New York: Schoken Books, 1993. Children's drawings and poems from Terezin Concentration Camp, 1942–44.

Wiesel, Eli. *Night.* New York: Hill and Wang, 1970. Autobiography of a boyhood in Auschwitz by the Nobel prizewinner for Peace in 1986. A literary and moving account.

* Yolen, Jane. *The Devil's Arithmetic*. New York: Puffin Penguin, 1990. A Holocaust "time" story about Hannah, who, during a Passover meal, opens the door to a Nazi pogrom in occupied Poland.

Ziemian, Joseph. *The Cigarette Sellers of Three Crosses Square*. New York: Avon Books. New material by Lerner Publications Company, 1975. Joseph Ziemian was a Jewish Resistance fighter who found a group of children who had escaped from the Warsaw Ghetto. This is the true story of their survival in hostile city streets. Translated from the Polish by Janina Baumann, whose book *Winter in the Morning* (Virago Press, 1986; Pan Books Ltd., 1987) is a touching commentary of Ghetto life and beyond, from the point of view of an adolescent girl.

ACKNOWLEDGMENTS

"Child Survivors" is from *Ghost Children*, copyright © 2000 by Lillian Boraks-Nemetz. First published by Ronsdale Press in 2000. Used by permission.

The excerpt from *Tell No One Who You Are: The Hidden Childhood of Régine Miller* is copyright © 1996 by Walter Buchignani. First published by Tundra Books in 1996. Used by permission.

"A Matter of Joy: The Story of Robert Krell" is from *Hidden Children: Forgotten Survivors of the Holocaust*, copyright © 1995 by André Stein. First published by Penguin Books in 1995. Used by permission of the author.

"Hide Me, Bubba Chaye" by Rachel Korn, translated by Seymour Levitan, is from *Paper Roses*, copyright © 1985 by Seymour Levitan. First published by Aya Press in 1985. Used by permission of the translator.

The excerpt from *Child of the Holocaust* is copyright © 1978 by Jack Kuper. First published by Paper Jacks Ltd. in 1978. Used by permission of the author.

"April 1943" is from *The Secret of Gabi's Dresser*, copyright © 1999 by Kathy Kacer. First published by Second Story Press in 1999. Used by permission of the publisher.

"In a Time of Terror: When Will Mother Return?" by René Goldman is used by permission of the author.

"I'm Fine" is from *Remember Me*, copyright © 2000 by Irene N. Watts. First published by Tundra Books in 2000. Used by permission.

"The Toy Steam Engine" by Serge (Wajnryb) Vanry is used by permission of the author.

"Holding Him" is copyright © 1999 by Deborah Schnitzer. First published in *CCL* 95, no. 25:3 (Fall 1999). Used by permission of the author.

The excerpt "A Blessing in Disguise" is from the play *None Is Too Many* by Jason Sherman (adapted from the book *None Is Too Many* by Irving Abella and Harold Troper), copyright © 1997 by Jason Sherman. Used by permission of the author.

"Tokyo, Japan, Winter 2000" and "Theresienstadt, May 1942" are from *Hana's Suitcase*, copyright © 2002 by Karen Levine. First published by Second Story Press in 2002. Used by permission of the publisher.

"Escape (Warsaw, 1942)" is from *The Old Brown Suitcase: A Teenager's Story of War and Peace*, copyright © 1994 by Lillian Boraks-Nemetz. First published by Ben Simon Publications in 1994. Used by permission.

The excerpt from *Children of Night* by Gabriel Emanuel is used by permission of the author.

"Romeo and Juliet in Suczorno" by Martha Blum is used by permission of the author.

"The Ghost Town of Kazimierz" is from *Ghost Children*, copyright © 2000 by Lillian Boraks-Nemetz. First published by Ronsdale Press in 2000. Used by permission.

"Mass Graves" is from *Violence and Mercy*, copyright © 1991 by Sarah Klassen. First published by Netherlandic Press in 1991. Used by permission of the author.

"Channel Crossing" from *The County of Birches*. Copyright © 1998 by Judith Kalman. Published in Canada by Douglas

& McIntyre. Reprinted by permission of the publisher.

"All There Is to Know about Adolph Eichmann" from *Stranger Music* by Leonard Cohen. Used by permission, copyright © Leonard Cohen.

"Stefan and Jesper" is from *Lisa*, copyright © 1984 by Carol Matas. First published by Lester and Orpen Dennys in 1984. Republished by Key Porter Books in 2002. Used by permission of Key Porter Books.

"Mr. Wallenberg" is from *My Canary Yellow Star*, copyright © 2001 by Eva Wiseman. First published by Tundra Books in 2001. Used by permission.

"The Plan" is from *A Time to Choose*, copyright © 1995 by martha attema. First published by Orca Book Publishers in 1995. Used by permission of the publisher.

"The Christmas Card" and "Love Is So Far Away" from *Letter from Vienna*. Copyright © 1995 by Claudia Cornwall. Published in Canada by Douglas & McIntyre. Reprinted by permission of the publisher.

The excerpt from *Goodbye Marianne* by Irene Kirstein Watts is copyright © 1994 by Irene Kirstein Watts. First published by Scirocco Drama in 1994. Used by permission.

The excerpt from "On Saint Katerine's Day" by Lili Berger, translated by Frieda Forman and Ethel Raicus, is from *Found Treasures: Stories by Yiddish Women Writers*. First published by Second Story Press in 1994. Used by permission.

"Shhh" is copyright © 1999 by Deborah Schnitzer. First published in *CCL* 95, no. 25:3 (Fall 1999). Used by permission of the author.

"The Holocaust and After," an excerpt from *Shovelling Trouble*, is used with permission of Mordecai Richler Productions Inc.

"Alien" is from *Snake Music*, copyright © 1978 by Kenneth Sherman. First published by Mosaic Press in 1978. Used by permission of the author.

The excerpt from *Assignment: Anne Frank*, an unpublished novel by Ellen Schwartz, is used by permission of the author.

The excerpt from "I Sat in Loews Theatre Staring at the Movie Screen" by Jean Little is from *Too Young to Fight*. Anthology copyright © 1999 by Priscilla Galloway. Reprinted by permission of Fitzhenry and Whiteside.

All survivor statements are used by permission of the individual survivors.